# Tax Myth Busters Don't Fall Prey to These Tax Misconceptions

### Exposing the Truths about the Top Tax Myths

## LILY TRAN

*FOREWORD BY DUKE ALEXANDER MOORE*

ISBN: 979-8-9857109-7-7

Editors: Leanne Kabat, Josh Burns, and Carol Pettit, EA

TaxUSign® is a registered Trademark
Printed in the United States of America
For more information, please visit us online at:
https://www.taxusign.com

# Disclaimer:

*Tax Myth Busters Don't Fall Prey to These Tax Misconceptions* does not provide binding tax, legal, or financial advice. The materials provided have been prepared for informational purposes only, and are not intended to provide tax, legal, or financial instructions as a substitute for a personal consultation. The material herein may not reflect the most current legislative or regulatory requirements, or the requirements of specific industries, or of specific states. These materials are not to be used for purposes of avoiding tax payments or tax penalties that may be imposed on a taxpayer. Readers should consult their own certified and professional tax, legal, and financial advisors before applying the laws or their interpretation of the laws to their specific situations

# Dedication

To my incredible clients.

Thank you for allowing me to be your trusted advisor and your main Tax Myth Buster on your path to prosperity.

# Acknowledgements

I want to thank Morris Armstrong, EA, who has been a mentor, friend, and a professional inspiration for years.

I want to thank Dave Saari, EA, Brad Messner, MBA, CBSA, and Steven D. Clifford, MDiv, CFP®, EA who has championed me and looked out for me on this incredible journey.

I want to thank my team, who have been incredible in supporting our clients all over the country, in all types of businesses. Your expertise and experience is so valued.

I want to give a heartfelt thank you to all the authors of this book. Duke, Al, Jessica, Matt, Jamie, Janet, and Fred, your tireless dedication to helping your clients has made the financial world a better place for all.

I want to thank Leanne Kabat for not only being with me every step of the way, but often showing me the way. You have generously encouraged me to rise to every next level, changing my business and my life. I'd be lost without you.

And finally, I want to acknowledge my daughter, Lucy. She is one of the bravest, more courageous spirits in my world, and she makes me strive to take more chances in my own life. Thank you for your fearlessness and humor, and for showing me how to show up fully in the world every day.

# Table of Contents

# Foreward

## By Duke Alexander Moore, EA

Welcome to "Tax Myth Busters Don't Fall Prey to These Tax Misconceptions." I'm excited to dive into this book with you and debunk some of the most common misunderstandings about taxes. Get ready to bust those myths wide open and gain a clearer understanding of how the tax world really works!

Taxes can be a daunting and confusing subject for many of us. We often hear all sorts of claims, rumors, and half-truths floating around, especially when it comes to maximizing deductions and minimizing our tax liabilities. But here's the thing: not everything you hear is true!

That's where this book comes in. We're here to separate fact from fiction, to empower you with accurate knowledge, and to arm you with the tools to navigate the complexities of the tax landscape. Together, we'll tackle common tax myths head-on, exposing the misconceptions that can lead us astray and potentially land us in hot water with the IRS.

Throughout the chapters, we'll dive deep into various tax topics, unravelling the truths and debunking the myths that have long persisted. From misunderstood deductions to misconceptions about business expenses, we'll shed light on the realities and equip you with the insights you need to make informed decisions about your taxes.

But hold on tight because this journey won't be all about debunking myths. We'll also provide practical tips, strategies, and best practices to help you optimize your tax planning, ensure compliance, and make the most of available deductions and credits. We want you to navigate the tax landscape with confidence and keep the most of your hard-earned money.

Remember, fam, knowledge is power when it comes to taxes. By busting these tax myths and gaining a clearer understanding of the rules and regulations, you'll be better equipped to make smart financial decisions and protect yourself from unnecessary risks.

So, let's get ready to challenge those misconceptions, arm ourselves with accurate information, and take control of our tax journey. Together, we'll become Tax Myth-Busters, setting the record straight and securing our fina - cial well-being.

Get ready to embark on this myth-busting adventure with "Tax Myth Busters Don't Fall Prey to These Tax Misconceptions." Let's smash those myths, unlock the truths, and empower ourselves to conquer the world of taxes with confidence

# Introduction

Entrepreneurs often start their businesses to provide a solution for ongoing problems they see in their world, gain professional freedoms, follow their passions, or build their future. Rarely do they start a business to pay a hefty tax bill, but that is often what happens because of the pervasiveness of tax myths and misconceptions. Whether you are an individual trying to navigate your tax obligations or a small business owner looking to comply with local, state, national, or international tax laws, having accurate information is essential. This book aims to bust the biggest tax myths and help entrepreneurs be compliant in their business ventures and avoid expensive and stressful tax issues.

This book draws on the latest research and opinions of experts in the field to provide clear and accurate information about taxes. It covers a wide range of topics, from basic tax concepts to more complex issues like get-rich-quick schemes, cryptocurrency, stocks, and tax evasion.

The authors in this book cover a wide range of tax topics and provide real-world examples so you can really see how believing these myths can cost you time, money, and your peace of mind. We don't want that for you, so let's dive in.

# Myth #1:
# "Get Rich Quick in the Digital World!"

## The Truth About Secret Formulas and Fast Money Online

*By Alexander J. Leruth, MBA, MAcc, EA, CPA, CMA*

The invention of the internet has led to a remarkable information economy. Consider the fact that we have more information available to us in a single web search than our ancestors had over the duration of their entire lives.

While the information economy has been a wonderful asset to entrepreneurs, the explosion of online business has also ushered in abundant opportunities for sneaky scammers to take advantage of unassuming newcomers.

It's an age-old problem.

From snake oil salesmen to call-center tech support cons, profitable markets have always attracted their share of fraudsters. Today, many online get-rich-quick schemes target aspiring entrepreneurs seeking guidance as they venture into very unfamiliar territory.

You've probably seen variations of such schemes floa - ing around online. Often, they're packaged in the form of courses, coaching groups, paid mentorships, or exclusive access to an influencer's inner circle

Before we move on, I want to make one thing clear: not all courses, coaching groups, mentorships, or paid resources are scams. The great power of the internet up to the present time has been the democratization of knowledge. The internet has largely eliminated historic obstacles to education, such as lack of wealth or status. The difference between a course offering tangible value and a scam disguised as an investment can be tough to discern. But you can look for the following:

- Mention of a secret formula to success that can only be acquired through that specific influencer or coach.
- Promises of quick financial wins, especially with minimal effort
- Claims that "anyone can do it."

Before investing in a digital course or coaching program, ask yourself, "Am I buying useful information, or am I buying into the marketing hype?"

Many online business influencers target driven individuals with a deep desire for financial success, but who might lack the business experience and digital instincts to discern legitimate business opportunities from online scams.

Consider dropshipping, for example. In traditional commerce, store owners purchase products for resale and store them in a warehouse or storage space.

But the internet has made it possible for eCommerce site owners to sell products they've never even seen in real life.

In this model, an eCommerce business owner identifies a marketable product and locates a source for the product—typically China. To sell the product, the business owner sets up an eCommerce shop via Shopify or a similar platform and lists the product for sale at a markup over the wholesale price. When a customer places an order, the seller buys the product directly from the wholesaler or manufacturer, who then ships the item directly to the customer. Ideally, after the initial business setup, the eCommerce owner makes a profit on each sale with just the click of a few buttons.

At first glance, it seems like an attractive business model.

It's low-risk, doesn't require space for inventory, doesn't require a physical storefront, and theoretically requires little capital to get started.

Just do an online search of "how to start a dropshipping business," and you'll find hundreds of articles with peppy titles like, *"How to Start a Dropshipping Business in 6 Easy Steps,"* and, *"Dropshipping for Dummies: Start Your Online Business Today!"*

These articles create an illusion of ease. They make the steps for starting an internet business seem straightforward and simple. The would-be dropshipper selects a business model, finds a source for their products, starts an online store, and suddenly they're in business! It's so easy anyone can do it, so the reader is told.

Often, these step-by-step articles are the first point in a sales funnel leading to a paid digital course in dropshipping.

One popular course website greets visitors with the heading, *"How to Earn 100K in 30 Days Dropshipping...Without Needing Any Experience!"* An aerial view of a catamaran gliding through turquoise Caribbean waters plays on a loop in the background. Below, a bright orange call-to-action button reads, "GET THE FREE TRAINING," in all caps.

If the sales sequence and promise are effecti e (and for hot leads, they usually are), the hopeful, aspiring business owner takes the bait and is now the proud owner of a $3,000 course and coaching membership led by a self-described expert in dropshipping.

### Getting Rich With the Internet

The proliferation of online money-making ventures like dropshipping and multi-level marketing companies (MLMs) has naturally generated a number of supposedly successful entrepreneurs who are willing and ready to help YOU earn 6-figures (or more) from the comfort of home... for a fee

These programs are usually advertised as having low startup costs, requiring no experience to start, and promising quick financial wins. These crafty folks often sell themselves with elaborate testimonials that artfully elicit a powerful emotional response in the prospect. These testimonials have been carefully crafted to get people to buy the programs or services by zeroing in on the aspiring entrepreneur's deep emotional desire for financial success and freedom.

Such programs are often taught by unqualified, unvetted people who more closely fit the definition of "infl - encer" than "entrepreneur." These influencers tend to sell publicly available, unoriginal, entry-level business content that is just repackaged concepts from other "coaches" and "mentors" in their industry.

Realistically, the coach may not even have work experience in the field they're purporting to have mastered. It's not unheard of for popular online business influencers to hire scriptwriters for their courses.

But, of course, these online business gurus aren't really selling courses. The background picture of a popular eCommerce coaching website, with a full-size picture of lush rice terraces of Bali accentuated by misty mountains says it all: This self-proclaimed guru is selling the dream of lifestyle. And for those aspiring business owners who lack the real-world experience to discern hype from real opportunity, it's easy to be persuaded to "buy in" for access to expertise.

It's an investment after all, isn't it?

**"How to Earn 100K in 30 Days"**
The great English poet Alexander Pope once wrote, "A little learning is a dangerous thing."

Many aspiring digital entrepreneurs have a hunger to learn and a drive for success. But their lack of practical knowledge pushes them to seek a mentor who can guide them. Unfortunately, the lack of information vetting on the internet makes it all too easy for business owners to buy the hype business influencers are selling. They believe the hype that raking in $100K a month with little to no effort is just around the corner. They fall for the claims that "anyone can do it" and that low startup costs mean they'll almost certainly turn a profit in record speed. They clearly see themselves standing on the shiny deck of that catamaran, the sun beaming down, living the good life.

Such entrepreneurs fall victim to the blind faith of naive optimism so commonly exploited by those selling internet get-rich-quick schemes. This credulity, in turn, renders the budding entrepreneur vulnerable to further programs and courses selling the dream of an easy win.

**Lies My Mentor Told Me**

Dropshipping, MLMs, and other creative internet schemes may theoretically offer nominal ways to make a little money online.

Do these internet businesses accomplish the big fina -cial wins they allude to in their marketing? Not typically. The course buyer, in fact, does not usually end up on a catamaran in the Caribbean.

But the consequence of the business owner's trust in whatever scheme they have bought into goes beyond the likelihood of small financial returns. With a confident and authoritative manner, online gurus often move beyond simple "how-to" courses and begin doling out business and financial advice to their followers. The only problem is—not all of these "coaches," "tax strategists," and "business gurus" have the necessary skills that they claim they do.

- *"Buy a new car and write it off as a business expense!*
- *"Just buy a decal for your vehicle. Then it counts as a business expense."*
- *"Employ your spouse on paper so you can write-off all of your meals."*
- *"Take a trip to Cancun with your employee/spouse and write it off! As long as you can show that you discussed business, it's fine.*

Although there are many so-called tax and fina - cial "pros" making a living giving advice on the internet, the IRS has very specific guidelines they use to determine what qualifies as a deduction and what does not. Section 162 of the Internal Revenue Code (IRC) addresses how to interpret business expenses. To qualify for a deduction, an expense must meet the following criteria:

1. It must be both ordinary and necessary.
2. If travel is involved, the travel must be necessary to carry on that specific trade or business. (The IRS keeps an extra close watch on travel expenses. If a claim wanders into extravagant territory, it's likely to be disallowed.)
3. If the expense could be considered a personal item, the taxpayer cannot benefit from that item beyond its business use.

If the expense meets these criteria, the IRS will request proof.

And if a business owner writes off questionable expenses on the advice of self-proclaimed internet experts, then they can't deliver acceptable documentation when tax season rolls around... the burden of proof is on the business owner to substantiate that the expenses were in fact deductible, or they will be the one paying the penalties.

Let's break down the car deduction as an example.

Can a car qualify as a legitimate tax deductible business expense, provided that it meets IRS criteria?

Yes.

But the problem is that the idea of a car write-off is tossed out by business coaches with no tax or financial education or qualifications, and they neglect to mention the fine print

Officia IRS guidelines state that when a car is used only for business purposes, the taxpayer may deduct the entire cost of ownership and operation.

If the car is used for both personal and business purposes, the taxpayer can only deduct the cost of the car's business use. This cost is calculated by dividing your total business miles by the total number of miles driven over the course of a year.

But there are caveats.

Understanding when a car is *fully deductible vs. not* can mean the difference between owning a company asset and being hit with a massive tax bill due to misinterpreting what a qualified business asset is. Imagine Quinn, the owner of an S Corporation, service-based business buys a large, premium SUV for $100K.

Quinn is the sole shareholder of the S Corp. They go to their rented office about 10 miles from home, three days a week. The SUV is their only vehicle, so they also use it in their daily personal life for running errands, driving their kids to and from school, and on weekend road trips. Quinn's business coach shares a couple of options for what they perceive as viable tax deductions.

**The Claim:** The business owner can deduct business miles.

**The Caveat:** Commuting miles don't count as business miles.

Quinn's business coach says they can deduct business miles driven to and from their offic during the previous year. But the business coach never mentioned that Quinn should have been keeping a mileage log or using mileage tracking software to discern what miles are deductible.

Quinn's coach is misinformed in two ways.

First, the IRS differentiates between commuting miles and business miles. If the business owner is driving from their home to their office this is considered a commute and is not tax deductible. If, however, they're logging miles driven between different business locations, like going on site visits or meeting with clients in-person, they can deduct those miles.

The second problem is that even if the miles were deductible, Quinn didn't keep a mileage log as required by the IRS, so there is no way to determine if business use was over 50%, which would allow for far greater deductions in the form of depreciation. This is likely what the business coach was incorrectly alluding to when mentioning "writing the SUV off."

**The Claim:** The business owner can buy the car for themselves, then add it to the books as a business asset.

**The Caveat:** Unless specific steps are followed, the business owner could find themselves having pierced the corporate veil by commingling business and personal funds.

In addition, at least one of two financial documents (loan agreement or accountable plan) need to be drafted and enacted before any commingling of funds could occur. These are rarely brought up by online business coaches or digital nomads as they are more complex for them to understand and implement. Piercing the corporate veil is a prohibited activity that could potentially lead to the S Corp election being revoked as well as open Quinn up to personal tax liability.

**The Claim:** Quinn can write off the entire $100K vehicle purchase by recording it on their S Corps' books as a business asset and taking the bonus depreciation deduction according to the business coach.

**The Caveat:** Unless Quinn keeps a proper mileage log or uses a mileage tracking software, they would not be eligible for bonus depreciation or know how much bonus depreciation, if any, they can be eligible for. Just following the business coach's recommendation would reduce their taxable income by $100,000, and under an IRS examination, Quinn would not be eligible for that deduction and would have to pay the significant underpayment of taxes, including all penalties and interest.

## The Reality

In truth, neither of the examples cited above would likely hold up in the event of an audit.

Should Quinn find themself in trouble with the IRS, they may believe that receiving incorrect tax advice from their coach will release them from liability. However, this is indeed false as Quinn would still be personally responsible as we discuss in the next section.

## The IRS Doesn't Care About Your Intentions

New business owners often find themselves operating from a place of misinformation regarding how the IRS approaches business deductions. It's not uncommon to find business owners who believe rendering a deduction valid in the eyes of the IRS is as simple as having the right intentions.

"If I get audited, I'll just tell the IRS auditor that I use my car for business," the logic goes. Except that's not how the IRS operates at all. The IRS works in numbers, facts, and data, not estimates and motives.

In the event of an audit, the IRS will require proof in the form of receipts, bank account information, and any other qualifying information as proof of the business's deductible expenses. In other words, simply calling a purchase a "business expense" won't do much if you are under examination with the Internal Revenue Service. They will want to see all requisite documentations showing what business was discussed to help them determine beyond a reasonable doubt if it should be deductible or not. And the onus is on you, the business owner, to provide that evidence.

## The Tax Problems that Arise When You Apply Bad Advice

As a financial professional, I've noticed that very few new business owners understand what it means to be tax compliant. They also struggle with practicing due diligence as they learn to handle taxes and finances as entrepreneurs

I've seen clients fail to vet the credentials of their tax preparer, which often leads to mistakes and erroneous filings. Even some EA, CPA, or tax attorneys who don't specialize in tax preparations can create havoc with a client's tax filings. I've also seen unethical tax professionals recommend extremely aggressive tax strategies that the IRS has already flagged as more likely than not of being fraudulent

And, as we're discussing in this chapter, I've seen plenty of inexperienced entrepreneurs blindly accept erroneous tax advice doled out by online business coaches and tax gurus.

And in truth, I get it. Starting a new business is exhilarating. When you're swept up in the moment of launching a lucrative dream into the world, who has time to worry about details like bookkeeping and tax records?

But these situations often end up with new business

owners acquiescing to perceived authority rather than thoroughly vetting tax and financial experts themsel es.

It's this susceptibility to influence that propagates and perpetuates incredibly negative surprises when tax season rolls around and the business owner finds that much of what they believed would be deductible actually is not.

Ultimately, the responsibility is on you, the business owner, to practice due diligence when it comes to taking and applying business and financial advice. At the end of the day, it's not your coach or mentor who is responsible for your tax bill—it's you. It's your business, your tax return, your records, and your signature on the dotted line.

*Myth Busted: "Get-Rich-Quick" Does Not Exist—and Blind Faith in Those Who Teach It Only Leads to Problems*

In many ways, the internet remains a modern Wild West—still largely unregulated and teeming with opportunities to strike gold. But those who are eager to take their chances in the online business world should keep an age-old truth in mind: nobody cares about you more than yourself.

Trusting e-courses, coaches, and gurus who preach the good news of how to get rich online usually leads to disappointment at best and financial hardship at worst. Danger lies not only in the "fast money" mindset pushed by online business influencers, but also in the notion that business owners can manipulate their way out of financial responsibilities (like paying taxes) with creative strategies.

In the end, you, the small business owner, must practice due diligence. Ask questions. Vet credentials, even if they sound impressive. Read the IRS Tax Code for yourself. Make it a point to understand different business structures so you can do what's best for your unique situation. Remember that just because somebody said something catchy on social media doesn't make it true.

And when tax season is upon us, remember that your accountant and the IRS don't care about what your business coach or favorite social media influencer has told you. Neither the IRS nor your tax pro consider tax hacks, trending hashtags, or viral videos substantial evidence.

We work in facts, numbers, and laws.

Is the fact that we carefully follow the guidelines set out by the Internal Revenue Code as alluring as the fantasies of wild riches and endless write-offs sold by online business influencers and digital nomads

Definitely not

But when you sign the dotted line on your tax return knowing you've done everything right, you'll be able to relax and continue moving your business forward confidently

## About the Author

### By Alexander J. Leruth, MBA, MAcc, EA, CPA, CMA

 Al Leruth works for a Top 10 accounting firm where he specializes in startups, SaaS, blockchain, and cryptocurrency. His work focuses on providing financial statements, financial planning & analysis, and managing communications around taxes or other special services.

Al has worked for companies like Apple, Target Mobile, and Bank of America where he used his background in finance, accounting, and technology consulting. He completed his MBA-Finance and became an Enrolled Agent (EA) in 2017. Al then started his business, Leruths, shortly after. Always striving for more knowledge, he enrolled and completed his Master of Accountancy (MAcc) in 2019. Al became a Certified Public Accountant (CPA) in 2021 and a Certified Management Accountant (CMA) in 2022.

Al values his role as a trusted advisor and advocate for his clients. He believes that by empowering his clients with education and timely information, he can help guide them to make the most informed, financially-healthy decisions that will allow them to comfortably navigate their future.

Company: Leruths
Website: https://leruths.com
Email: al@leruths.com
Phone: 651-252-4029

# Myth #2:
## "Be an Influencer and Deduct Everything!"

## The Truth About Tax Write-offs and Fake Promises

*By Jessica Smith, EA*

As a tax professional, I see a lot of bad tax advice floating around in the digital ether.

*Buy a car so you can write off the interest*

*Don't report money from your side business—the IRS will never know!*

*Book that trip to Italy! As long as you're working a little while you're there, it counts as a tax write-off*

The ever-changing nature of tax law and our fast-paced information economy have combined into a perfect storm of fast-spreading inaccurate tax advice.

And the so-called "influencer" community is one of the worst for this phenomenon.

I've seen an emerging trend among social media infl - encers in recent years.

These Insta-stars, primarily young, attractive women, who are making a living off their own personality-based brands, mistakenly believe they're free to claim anything and everything remotely related to their businesses as a tax deduction.

The appeal of this mentality is obvious: who wouldn't want to have the freedom to write off their wardrobe, beauty care, restaurant meals, and travel expenses?

Here's an example of the erroneous influencer tax-logic I see: A lifestyle guru purchases items for "clothing hauls" on her YouTube channel. She spends $1,000 on clothing and accessories from Target, believing she can write off the expense. It's related to her business, isn't it?

Sure, it's related.

But there's a distinct difference between something "related" to a business and a qualifiable business expense, as discussed in this chapter.

If you own a business, especially one that blurs the fine line between your job and your lifestyle, it's essential to understand the difference bet een the two.

**If It Sounds Too Good To Be True...**

Are social media influencers particularly interested in spreading tax misinformation? Are they invested in a secret anti-tax cabal hellbent on tricking people into itemizing fake deductions?

Not exactly.

But the soundbite, fast-take, Insta-everything internet culture of today creates an environment ripe for misinformation.

Here are a few examples of tax lies I've seen spread across the internet in recent years:

- YouTubers do clothing hauls on their channels to

write off the clothing on their taxes. Because making the video is considered work, they can write off their clothes!

- Instagram stars can write off travel expenses when they fly around the world for photo shoots. Tax-free travel? Yes, please.
- Working from a home office as an influencer means you can write off your entire mortgage payment! What an amazing tax hack!
- Tax-free clothes?
- Travel?
- Writing off our entire mortgage payment?

You don't say!

Here's a list of things I'd love to deduct from my taxes next year:

- Designer clothing (to look great on my Zoom calls).
- Yearly Botox (to look extra great on my Zoom calls).
- Mani-pedis (hangnails get in the way of data entry).
- Weekly massages (to manage anxiety during tax season).
- A trip to Bora Bora (to decompress after tax season).

All I have to do is demonstrate a tiny connection between these items and my business, and I'm off the hook on taxes?

Done!

It sounds ridiculous, but it's shocking how many people fall for this "anything-goes-as-a-business-expense" mentality.

The result for me as a tax professional isn't just getting a good laugh over the wacky things people sometimes try to write off In recent years, I've increasingly found myself helping misguided small business owners clean up tax messes caused by misinterpretation of eligible business deductions.

These messes could often have been avoided completely with quality research or consulting a certified tax pro

## The Myth of the Never-ending Write-Offs

Have you heard that it counts as a write-off as long as you use your boat to entertain clients?

Or that your vacation to Cabo counts as long as you checked your email while you were there?

The misguided notion that simply filing an LLC or incorporating your business can minimize, or even eliminate, your tax bill is responsible for many of the financial mistakes I see young business owners make.

Here's the reality about tax write-offs

IRS Publication 535 explains the types of expenses that are eligible as business deductions.

To be deductible, a business expense must be both ordinary and necessary.

An ordinary expense is something commonly used in a specific industry. For example, wire cutters for an electrician or hair stylist insurance for a salon owner.

A necessary expense is helpful and appropriate for that

specific industry

I'd be lying if I didn't admit there's lots of room for interpretation, especially for a job like social media influence that blurs the line between personal and business expenses.

For example, imagine an influencer running an online fitness business. She regularly records and uploads fitness videos, offers private consulting services, and has promotional deals with several supplement companies.

Some business items she's purchased in the last year include workout clothing, filming equipment, a new yoga mat, and a membership to an online bookkeeping platform. For personal maintenance, she has also had her hair highlighted at the salon and had Botox injections.

A good way to answer whether a purchase is both ordinary and necessary is to ask, "Could one realistically perform the actions necessary for running this business without that purchase?"

One could make a reasonably strong case that her clothing, workout equipment, and bookkeeping platform fees are vital for running her business.

As an influencer, it also makes sense for her to prioritize personal maintenance. After all, an argument could be made that maintaining a pleasing physical appearance for the camera is both an ordinary and necessary expense in the world of influencin .

But U.S. tax court precedent has shown time and time again that personal expenses don't qualify as business deductions.

## No, You Can't Write Off Your Botox

The confusion about what is and isn't an allowable business deduction often results from trying to interpret vague IRS guidance as a layperson. This is how we end up with social media influencers claiming they can write off shopping sprees, breast augmentation, and Botox treatments without a care in the world.

When dealing with questionable purchases, considering how much business use versus personal use an item will get is helpful.

Here's the breakdown of how the IRS is likely to view the average influencer's purchases

### Clothing

Can an influencer purchase a new wardrobe and write it off under the name of photo shoots or clothing hauls? Not if she's wearing the clothes for social media photos or videos and then hanging them up in her closet for personal use.

What about specialty clothing for a specific job? Are yoga pants an eligible deduction for a yoga teacher? At first glance, you'd think that a yoga teacher buying a pair of Lululemon pants would clearly be considered ordinary and necessary.

But the IRS, aware of the potential for abuse of a policy permitting clothing deductions, has a caveat about work clothes.

They must be required for employment and not generally recognized as acceptable streetwear.

So, with great sadness for YouTube yoga gurus, I announce the truth: your stretchy yoga pants don't count. I'm sorry.

*Travel*

What about those fabulous Instagram shots that garner millions of likes and lucrative sponsorships?

Can an influencer hop a plane to the newest "it" destination, take a few photos, then spend a week on the beach, calling it a tax write-off

Definitely not

For travel to be tax deductible, specific criteria must be met:

1.  The individual must be traveling away from where she regularly does business.
2.  She needs to prove that most of her time in that location was spent in the pursuit of business.

A trip to an influencer marketing event in Bangkok spent in meetings, seminars, and networking sessions would likely meet the criteria of ordinary and necessary.

A trip to Santorini spent taking photos for Instagram, while possibly relevant to a lifestyle brand, is drifting into "lavish or extravagant" territory. The IRS clearly states in Topic Number 511 that expenses considered extravagant are not eligible for deduction.

*Meals*

Here's a silver lining about business purchases: 50% of business meals are deductible, with a couple of caveats.

In most cases, the 50% meal deduction applies when meeting with a client for business purposes. But why can't you write off the entire meal? Because the IRS wants to make sure you can fairly deduct your client's meal, but they don't want to give business owners too much leeway when it comes to dining out. Permitting a 100% deduction would likely inspire more creative write-offs than the IRS wants to deal with. To qualify for this deduction, you need a receipt detailing the client's name and a description of the meeting's purpose.

So, an influencer simply taking a photo to post before diving into her bougie shrimp tacos won't have a legitimate deductible expense unless her documentation proves the meal's purpose as a business expense.

*Gym Membership*

Can a non-fitness-related influencer deduct gym fees because she wants to stay in shape for the camera? No, she cannot.

Personal maintenance expenses are very hard to pass off as legitimate business expenses. Listing them gives the IRS a good reason to take an extra close look at your books.

Gym fees can potentially be tax-deductible in fields wherein maintaining a certain fitness level is vital to the job, like a personal trainer, bodybuilder, or an actor training for a role.

Again, "ordinary and necessary" are the key to keep in mind.

*Botox*

It shouldn't be surprising that cosmetic treatments to solely improve physical appearance don't count as deductions.

One could argue that personal beauty maintenance expenses like Botox and fillers are essential to running an influencer business. After all, don't influencers need to look good for their audiences?

Sure, but Botoxing crow's feet isn't objectively necessary for them to perform their jobs.

So, when social media influencers claim they can write off cosmetic treatments, don't believe them—it's simply not true.

No matter what the internet tells you, I promise that influencers have not found a magical tax loophole that allows everything beautiful and good to count as a write-off.

Not even Hollywood celebrities, who make their money by building a personal and professional brand based (mostly) around their physical appearances and (questionable) acting abilities, are allowed to deduct personal maintenance expenses. The overlap with personal expenses is just too much.

So how does the IRS make a determination about an expense's eligibility as a business deduction?

First, they'll determine whether the expense is allowable under Section 162 of the Internal Revenue Code (I.R.C.) They'll ask:

- Is the expense ordinary and necessary?
- Are any travel expenses needed to carry on a specific trade or business? Do those expenses cover basic travel, or would they be considered extravagant if using the "sniff test"
- If the expense is needed for business but could fall into the "personal maintenance and care" category, is the individual taxpayer benefiting from that item beyond its business use? If "yes," then it cannot be deducted.

If, after checking for these criteria, you find that the expense isn't allowable, tough luck.

But if the expense is allowed, the IRS will next determine whether the business records satisfy tax code requirements for a deduction.

They'll want to see sufficient evidence that

A. The expense in question is worth its declared value,

B. There's a record with the *time and place* the item was used,

C. There is a real business purpose for the expense, and

D. The business relationship between the taxpayer and the...

I'm not clear on how to finish this sentence. The exact

28

text from 274 is, "the business relationship to the taxpayer of the person receiving the benefit." But because we are discussing influencers who ARE taxpayers, I'm confused about how this part of the audit technique would apply.

Ok, so the relationship this is referring to is the infl-encer (taxpayer) and anyone who may also benefit from the expense.

For example, if I take you out to lunch and we discuss the copywriting for my book chapters, we can confirm our relationship has a business purpose. Now let's say that I take my husband with me to meet with you over lunch where you and I discuss my book chapters. Aside from being arm candy, what business purpose does it serve for him to be present? Likely none. It's common for people to assume you can take a regular expense such as a vacation or a night out and magically convert it to a business expense because you "discussed business" with someone or answered emails. The primary reason for the incurring expense has to be for a business purpose and not just something you would do on any other day of the week if you didn't have a business.

There's this woman on Instagram claiming to be a tax coach but her videos often cross the line of helpfulness and even legality. Her advice is all about taking ordinary, every-day expenses and "converting" them to business expenses. In one example, she posted a video discussing how to write off a trip to Disney because you recorded content there— which is false information, but people eat her content up without verifying its validity. I share sites with my clients based on facts and the law, and how tricks like the ones this woman shares don't work and can land someone in hot water. Rant over!

## Myth Busted: No, Social Media Influencers Cannot Write Off Anything They Want

As a tax pro, it's fascinating to watch how our culture's ideas of business shift over time.

Twenty years ago, it would have been hard to imagine that there would someday be job categories like "podcaster," "vlogger," and "influencer.

Tax laws will undoubtedly have to be updated to adequately address dynamic changes to the novel businesses the internet has helped create.

Will we someday see a U.S. tax code that allows internet-based celebrities to write off their MediSpa treatments, travel, and personal trainer fees in the name of brand investment?

Probably not, but the future's open to change.

Until then, I'll keep designing tax-saving strategies for ambitious small business owners.

Just don't ask me to write off  our Botox.

# About the Author

## Jessica Smith, EA

Jessica L. Smith, EA is a speaker and educator with more than a decade of experience helping small business owners overcome their tax problems and leveraging the federal tax code to save thousands in income taxes. As an Enrolled Agent, she has earned the privilege of representing taxpayers before the Internal Revenue Service. She is a candidate for admission to practice before the United States Tax Court as a non-attorney.

She is a member of the National Association of Enrolled Agents, the National Association of Tax Professionals, and the Idaho Association of Tax Consultants. Jessica earned a Bachelor of Science in Accounting, summa cum laude from California College.

Jessica's practice focuses on implementing tax reduction strategies and representing taxpayers before the Internal Revenue Service. In 2022, she founded The 100K EA where she guides enrolled tax practitioners through the ins and outs of resolving complex tax problems.

Company: Tax Savvy Jessica, LLC
Website: https://taxsavvyjessica.com/
Email: jessica@taxsavvyjessica.com
Phone: 619-494-1040

# Myth #3:
## "I Lost Money in Stocks So I Don't Need to Report It."

### The Truth About Capital Losses

*By Matthew Gaylor, EA, CTC, CTP*

In this chapter, the myth we are busting is if an asset is sold for a loss, then that transaction is not required or beneficial to be reported on a tax return. In my practice, I have heard this phrase, or a similar one, many times: "I sold stocks (or another asset) at a loss so that transaction doesn't need to be reported on the tax return". The frequency that I hear this myth indicates that many people believe it to be true. But where did this myth come from, and why is it not accurate?

It is difficul to pinpoint an origin for this myth but based on conversations with clients, I have found there are several underlying beliefs that lead to the spreading of this myth, which will be discussed in this chapter. Let's first define capital gains and losses under the tax l ws.

From the IRS:

"Almost everything you own and use for personal or investment purposes is a capital asset. Examples include a home, personal-use items like household furnishings, and stocks or bonds held as investments. When you sell a capital asset, the difference between the adjusted basis in the asset and the amount you realized from the sale is a capital gain or a capital loss. Generally, an asset's basis is its cost to the owner. You have a capital gain if you sell the asset for more than your adjusted basis. You have a capital loss if you sell the asset for less than your adjusted basis. Losses from the sale of personal-use property, such as your home or car, aren't tax deductible" (Topic No. 409 Capital Gains and Losses. https://www.irs.gov/taxtopics/tc409).

The general rule is that a capital gain or loss is realized when an asset is sold, and the gain or loss is determined by the cost of that asset subtracted from the sale price.

An example using stock: sell 1 share of Apple stock for $145 that was originally purchased for $175, that results in a $30 loss. That example is straightforward as the stock was bought for $175 but there can be complications in calculating the cost of the asset, referred to as the basis, if it was not acquired in a purchase. Some examples of these complications include if the stock or asset was inherited, received as a gift, received as payment for services rendered or if the asset was used in a trade or business such as a rental property.

Discussion of these special circumstances are vast and beyond the topic of this chapter, so they will not be discussed further here. If you believe a special circumstance may apply, please reach out to myself or another author of this book.

Now that we have a foundation for how a loss is determined, let's look at some of the reasons I have observed as to why it is believed that a loss shouldn't be reported:

- Stock sales are reported on tax forms 1099 so the IRS already knows about the losses,
- Misunderstanding of how a stock/asset loss impacts the tax return and ability to lower the tax liability,
- Loss in value (unrealized losses) are not deductible and the mistaken belief that a realized loss (actual sale resulting in a loss) is not deductible,
- Transactions involving crypto currency (like Bitcoin, Ethereum, Shiba, etc.),
- Embarrassment in having lost money on investments,
- Or personal asset losses are non-deductible so that applies to all loss transactions.

The above is not an exhaustive list but are sentiments that have been commonly and repeatedly expressed in conversations with clients. Let's dive into these items and work to understand them better.

**Stock sales and tax form 1099**

Investment brokers and custodians report the sale of stocks, bonds and mutual funds on tax form 1099-B. That tax form reports important information such as the security's name, sale proceeds and the date of the sale and beginning in 2011, these tax forms have added sections or boxes titled "Transactions for which basis is being reported to the IRS" and "Transactions for which basis is not being reported to the IRS". As those descriptions indicate, the brokers are reporting to the IRS the cost basis of securities sold, or not.

When the cost basis is reported to the IRS, this assists in calculating the gain or loss on these sales transactions.

But confusion about the phrase "not being reported to the IRS" has led some taxpayers to believe the entire transaction is not being reported to the IRS and can avoid being reflected on their income tax return filing, especially when there is a loss reflected on these tax forms

This misunderstanding has led clients of tax professionals to believe they are being helpful by not providing this seemingly unnecessary information at tax time because it was "not reported to the IRS". In actuality, the information that was not reported was the cost basis of the sold stock, bond or mutual fund. The IRS still receives the sales proceed amounts and is comparing that information to the filed tax return

Without the cost basis, the IRS is left to assume the sale resulted in a gain as they don't have any information reported to them to dispute that assumption.

As you can imagine, omission of income generates a letter from the IRS proposing the assessment of additional tax. In order to dispute the taxes, that notice requires a response to provide additional information to the IRS.

For most people, a letter from the IRS causes panic and stress, and in order to reduce the possibility of receiving notices from the IRS, it is important to ensure that transactions reported on tax forms 1099 be captured in reporting on the income tax return.

Additionally, Congress has instructed the IRS to require additional reporting via form 1099 for transactions that include the sale of digital assets (an example of this would be cryptocurrency like Bitcoin) or the use of payment processors (like PayPal). Transactions reported to the IRS on these forms will also need to be reported on tax returns to reduce inquiries and correspondence from the IRS. Cryptocurrency transactions will be discussed again later in this chapter.

**"The result is a loss, why bother reporting?"**
The topic of this chapter is about capital losses, but it may be helpful to know that capital gains and losses are a specific category of income for tax purposes

The sale of stocks, bonds, mutual funds, other investments, and/or capital assets results in capital gains or loss. Capital assets receive special treatment on tax returns, for example capital gains are taxed at lower rates for long term asset sales (assets sold after being owned for 1 year or longer).

But why bother reporting capital losses? What benefits do capital losses provide? Capital losses can be used first to offset capital gains (both short term and long term) up to the amount of realized losses for the year. This is a reduction of capital gain income and results in a reduction of tax.

If there are capital losses that exceed capital gains, the excess amount up to $3,000 per year can be used to offset other income, which could result in tax savings of up to $1,110 at the top Federal tax rate. If there are losses more than this amount, they can be carried over to the following year to offset capital gains in that year or used up to $3,000 per year.

Here is an example to illustrate:

Beth bought stock in a prior year for $25,000, and in 2023 that same stock is sold for $15,000. The result is a long-term capital loss of $10,000. In 2023, Beth also sold another stock that had a gain of $6,000.

On her 2023 tax return, she would report the two stock transactions separately, and the net result would be an overall loss of $4,000.

For 2023, she would be able to deduct $3,000 on her tax return to lower her income by that amount and carry forward the remaining $1,000 to be used in 2024.

From the above example, the benefit of the loss is the current year's reduction in income, first by offsetting the gain from the sale of the second stock and next by being allowed a $3,000 deduction against other income for that year. The excess is then going to be allowed as a deduction in the next year, providing a future benefit to Beth

If Beth had not reported the loss transaction, then her income would have been overstated and result in paying more tax than necessary both in 2023 and again in 2024. The reporting of this transaction is necessary to benefit from experiencing a loss on the tax return.

Having a loss that results in a carryover provides the opportunity to plan in the following year to sell a capital asset with a gain and minimize the tax impact of that transaction.

**"My investment is down in value, that's a tax write off"**
Through the years, I have seen financial bubbles in the stock markets, real estate, and recently in cryptocurrency. When these downturns have occurred, inevitably the question is asked: "Can I write off the loss suffered in my account?" The details behind that question are important to determine if there is a tax deduction available.

Often the question is really asking about the decline in value of the asset and not the result of a sale of the asset, referred to as a realized loss. Many taxpayers, after being told they can't deduct a loss due solely to decline in value, believe that they are unable to later take a loss once they realize the actual loss through a sales transaction.

Another confusing situation is when the financial account is a retirement account (for example IRAs or 401(k) accounts) that experiences a loss in value. Transactions involving retirement accounts do not generate capital gains or losses but result in ordinary income tax treatment, when withdrawals are taken from these accounts. And again, when clients are told this account decrease in value does not provide a current tax deduction, that can be misunderstood to apply to other investment accounts, which is not the case for non-retirement accounts when investment holdings were sold for a loss. If an investment account has experienced a decrease in value, there may be an opportunity to implement a tax strategy referred to as "stock loss harvesting." This strategy is where losing stock positions (or other assets) are sold to generate a capital loss that can be used to offset other capital gains. This may be useful to do in the same year in which a large gain is expected (and realized) and there are specific investments that have decreased in value and are no longer desired to be held in your fina - cial portfolio. This strategy should be reviewed with your financial and tax advisors to determine if it would be beneficial in your specific situation, as timing is critical to be able to effecti ely implement this strategy.

**Cryptocurrency Transactions**

Another capital asset to discuss is cryptocurrency (crypto), or digital assets. The best-known example of cryptocurrency is Bitcoin, which has been around since 2008, but there are hundreds of different cryptocurrencies available for investment using platforms such as Coinbase.

There are many ways to obtain crypto, such as a purchase via an online platform, mining (using computer resources to verify transactions related to a specific crypto and being compensated in that process), receiving crypto as payment for goods or services (some businesses accept this as payment), and various other ways.

The treatment of the receipt of crypto and the related tax treatment of that transaction is not our topic here, but it does affect the calculation of a gain or loss

The purchase or receipt of the crypto is usually going to

be the cost basis of that asset. As we covered earlier in this chapter, the difference between the sale price and basis will be the calculation for gain or loss, which will be reported on the tax return.

A "sale" for purposes of cryptocurrency can occur in many ways—an actual sale on a platform or exchange, like Coinbase; a conversion from one asset to another (for example trading Bitcoin for Ethereum); or remitting cryptocurrency as payment for goods and services (for example, using a crypto "wallet" to purchase coffee results in a reportable capital gain or loss transaction).

These examples of sales are not exhaustive but merely used to illustrate potential transactions that could result in reporting on a tax return. With expanded reporting requirements in recent tax legislation, this list will continue to grow.

At the time of writing this chapter, crypto assets have suffered significant decline in values in part to the failing of crypto exchanges, the result is that some assets have decreased in value to practically zero. Unfortunately, no loss can be reported on the tax return unless the specific cryptocurrency was actually sold or converted from one type of asset to another, as discussed previously. The IRS has released guidance on these specific situations and their position is no loss is recognized until the asset is disposed of.

In general, for a taxpayer to benefit from losses in crypto transactions: first, the crypto asset must be deemed to be held for investment purposes (or part of a trade or business), and second, an event that results in either a sale or exchange of that asset occurs. Absent those two criteria being met, the loss is not reportable on the tax return.

**"A loss from a personal use property is not deductible."** Earlier the definition of a capital asset was provided from the IRS website: "Almost everything you own and use for personal or investment purposes is a capital asset." It is accurate to say that a loss from the sale of personal use property, like a car or home, is not deductible.

During the Great Recession, many people were selling their personal residences at a loss compared to the purchase price of that home. The loss from those sales would result in no tax deduction being allowed for the sale of a personal residence. Many taxpayers have been told that a loss incurred from the sale of a personal use property does not allow a deduction and have assumed that to be the case for sales of other items on a broader scale.

Due to that assumption, many people have lost potential tax deductions by not discussing the sale transaction with their tax advisor to determine if the item was personal use or not.

Consulting with a tax advisor prior to the sale of an asset provides the opportunity to identify if the asset is personal use (not tax deductible) or may qualify as an investment asset (and resulting loss eligible for tax deduction).

For example, an automobile that is purchased and used in everyday life is generally going to be a personal use asset and the sale of that vehicle, if sold at a loss, would not qualify as a deductible capital gain (although, during the COVID pandemic, many people were able to sell their vehicles at a gain, that gain would be reportable as a taxable gain, but I digress from my point).

In contrast, some individuals purchase vehicles as a collection. For example, in the Phoenix/Scottsdale, Arizona area, there is an annual Barrett-Jackson auto auction where classic and collectible cars are bought and sold.. If a vehicle is purchased with the intent of selling it after it has appreciated in value, that may provide sufficien  purpose to allow a loss to be tax deductible.  The determination is based on the facts and circumstances surrounding the transaction and careful planning and documentation may uncover an opportunity to reduce taxes in the form of a capital loss deduction.

**Summary**

We have looked at the myth that there is no benefit to reporting a loss from the sale of assets on the income tax return. The origin of this myth has many different sources, such as the belief that the result was a loss so there is no benefit, or reason to report that activity, or the 1099 forms report the information to the IRS why do I need to put it on my tax return, or after being told that a decrease in value doesn't affect the tax return but that does not apply to realized losses (actual loss transactions in non-retirement accounts), or handling of reporting of cryptocurrency or transactions or sales of personal use property.

It is important to report the sale of a capital assets on your tax return 1) to reduce potential notices from the IRS proposing additional tax for not matching the information they have received, and 2) to reduce taxable income for capital losses ( otherwise taxes may be paid in excess of the required amount).

The situations surrounding reporting of these transactions can be complicated and if you lack confidence that you are able to report correctly, please seek professional advice from a trusted tax professional.

## About the Author

### Matt Gaylor, EA, CTC, CTP

Matt has been serving clients in tax compliance, planning and resolution as owner of Gaylor Tax Services LLC since 2004. Matt obtained his bachelor's degree in accounting from the University of Arizona, later obtained his Enrolled Agent credential (authorization to represent taxpayers before the IRS), and received his Certified Tax Coach (CTC) and Certified Tax Planner (CTP) designations through the American Institute of Certified Tax Planners (AICTP).

In 2022, Matt was selected from his peers at the AICTP as member of the year. Matt is also a member of these professional organizations: the National Association of Enrolled Agents (NAEA) and the National Association of Tax Professionals (NATP). Through his experience, Matt has learned that preventing IRS notices for unreported transactions is a crucial way to successfully navigate the backlogged IRS system and stays mindful of the sports mantra: "the best offense is a good defense." Successfully implementing legal tax strategies requires action before the tax filing season because good tax planning is a year-round commitment.

Company: Gaylor Tax Services LLC
Website: www.gaylortax.com
Email: matt@gaylor.tax

# Myth #4:
## "An S Corp Is a Tax-Saving Machine."

## The Truth About S Corps

### By Jamie E. O'Kane, CPA

You are here for tax misconceptions, and this here is the one that I run into most often:

*S Corporations are tax-savings machines. Just start one! It's easy.*

Day in and day out we meet business owners who haven't made a dime in revenue but are somehow the sole share-holders of a shiny new S Corporation. These business owners find themselves having to understand the compliance require-ments needed to maintain their S Corporation as well as the costs to do so after the deed is done—usually starting their business in the red on time, energy, and money.

I am here to break it down for you so that if you are thinking of taking the S Corporation route you have a better foundation of knowledge. This knowledge can help you make the right choice for you and your business and help you un-derstand what the heck your tax professional may be talking about. Hopefully. I will do what I can.

Let's get into it.

What is an S Corporation?

S Corporations are corporations that elect to pass corpo-rate income, losses, deductions, and credits through to their shareholders for federal tax purposes. Shareholders of S Corporations report the fl w-through of income and losses on their personal tax returns and are assessed tax at their individual income tax rates. This allows S Corporations to avoid double taxation on the corporate income.

Basically, S Corps are sort of a hybrid entity of a C Corp and a partnership/sole proprietorship. The S Corp takes aspects of both of those entity types and makes some of the compliance simpler and some more difficult Welcome to the U.S. tax code.

Most people establish S Corps as a tax savings move but don't understand the compliance requirements they are taking on. So, before we talk potential tax savings, let's talk compliance. I will take you through the biggest considerations to understand before you leap.

**Paying Yourself Can Be Complicated**

Let's get to the most pertinent subject first—p ying yourself. You are in business to make money and you would like to use said money to fund your business and, most importantly, personal goals. If you are a shareholder in an S Corporation you can't just take any and all available cash at any given time. There are compliance issues and considerations when taking each and every dollar out of the S Corp. There are a few ways to get money out of an S Corporation. Here are the most common:

1. Reasonable Compensation
2. Dividend Distributions

3. Expense Reimbursements

4. Shareholder Loans

All of these have considerations to understand before implementing. Let's break it down.

**Reasonable Compensation**

S Corporation shareholders who work for or provide services to the S Corp are required to be paid a reasonable W-2 wage. This salary needs to be a proper and defensible amount that considers the roles, tasks, and expertise that the shareholder provides as an employee of the corporation. There are many ways to determine what a proper salary would be for each shareholder. Some of the most common approaches are below:

**Many Hats Approach**—this type of analysis takes the roles, tasks, or "hats" a shareholder wears in the business, allocates them over the hours the shareholder dedicates to the business and then assigns a market wage to come up with a composite salary. This approach is most commonly used for small businesses whose shareholders provide a myriad of services to the S Corp.

**Market Approach**—this type of analysis determines the salary required to hire a replacement for the shareholders' role.

Which approach should a shareholder use? It depends, but the goal here is always to determine the minimum salary that is reasonable and defensible in the event of an audit. Let's do an example to illustrate the difference between each approach:

The sole shareholder is a veterinarian with 10+ years of experience whose S Corporation provides in-home euthanasia and end-of-life services in the Denver Metro area. The shareholder is the only employee, and they work full-time. Each week the shareholder's roles include bookkeeping, payroll, supply purchases, scheduling appointments, driving, and veterinary services. Each approach produces the following compensation:

Many Hats Approach - $80,000 annually

Market Approach - $117,000 annually

In this scenario the shareholder has many roles that are valued at a lower market wage than their main professional role. The many hats approach takes these roles into account while the market approach does not. In this scenario the shareholder would likely choose to document the lower salary as their minimum reasonable compensation. The shareholder can always take more salary in the event they want to maximize retirement contributions, are looking to show more W-2 income for investment purposes, etc.

Takeaway: What would reasonable compensation be for each shareholder who actively works in the business?

**Dividend Distributions**

Dividend distributions are payments of retained profits, cash, or property to the shareholders. The S Corporation must pay the distributions in proportion to each shareholder's stock ownership. Failure to do so invalidates the S Corp status and reverts the entity to a C Corp. Hooray! Double taxation.

Every single S Corp shareholder I take on as a client gives me a funny look when I say "okay, let me show you how to know how much cash the S Corp can distribute without creating a taxable event."

Then they say: "I can't just take whatever is in the bank account?"

Unfortunately, no. Anytime an S Corp distributes cash or property in excess of a shareholder's basis (we will get to basis in a bit) in the S Corp, the distributions are taxable.

How does an S Corp have available cash in excess of profits? Debt. Debt such as credit card liabilities, lines of credit, operating loans and even shareholder loans to the S Corp create cash in excess of profits

Property distributions are distributions of capital assets, inventory, investments, etc. These types of distributions can be complicated so I will just say: don't distribute property out of an S Corp to shareholders without talking to your tax professional.

Takeaway: Be very cautious when distributing cash or property to shareholders.

### Expense Reimbursements

Shareholders who provide services to their S Corps usually have out-of-pocket expenses or personal assets they use for their business's benefit. The most common are home offices, vehicle use, licenses, travel, etc. Because S Corporation shareholders are also employees these expenses must be properly reimbursed to be deductible. Enter the accountable reimbursement plan.

An accountable reimbursement plan is a plan that qualifies under IRS regulations to not be included in the employee's taxable income. These plans require that all expenses be legitimate business expenses and that they be documented (receipts, mileage logs, etc.). After those qualifications are met the reimbursement dollars are tax free.

Takeaway: Establish an accountable plan to be paid tax free dollars from your S Corp.

## Shareholder Loans

Shareholders and their S Corps can loan each other money. These transactions have certain requirements to make sure they are legitimately loans instead of compensation to the shareholder, distributions, contributions, gifts, etc. These requirements include:

- a contract with a stated interest rate
- a specified length of time for rep yment, and
- a consequence for failure to repay the loan

If a transaction is truly a loan, it should look and act like any other business loan.

Takeaway: Loan agreements are always a good idea.

## Shareholder Basis & Why It's Required

Basis is the value of a shareholder's investment or stock at any given time. Basis is used for tax purposes to determine if dividend distributions are taxable, if the shareholder can deduct losses, and to determine gain or loss on their investment in the event of a sale.

Up until a few years ago basis was required to be tracked by the shareholder in their recordkeeping and wasn't required to be included in their tax filings. This requirement is one of the most overlooked compliance pieces by shareholders and, unfortunately, their tax professionals.

As of 2018, the IRS now requires basis schedules to be included with the personal tax return any time a shareholder reports a loss, receives a distribution, disposes of stock, or receives a loan payment. This requirement catches most S Corp shareholders into the required basis reporting each year.

Takeaway: S Corp shareholders must track their basis and report it.

### Bookkeeping, Payroll & Tax Filings

### Bookkeeping

Bookkeeping is an essential part of running any business, but it is especially important when maintaining an S Corporation. S Corps are entities separate from their shareholders and therefore documenting each transaction properly for reporting and compliance purposes is of the utmost importance. Proper books and records inform tax filings, lending decisions, available capital and managerial decisions.

The elements of a proper bookkeeping system are bookkeeping software, frequent updating, record retention and periodic verification of balances

Bookkeeping software—this is the cornerstone of any bookkeeping system. Software maintains double-entry accounting for each transaction which then provides the availability of financial reportin .

Frequent updating – bookkeeping should never be a once-a-year task. Monthly updates and reconciliations should be done to maintain balances, understand trends and make decisions.

Record Retention – all businesses should maintain receipts, invoices, purchase orders, bills, payroll reports, etc. Digital filing is recommended

Verification of Balances – entering transactions into bookkeeping software isn't enough to have accurate bookkeeping. The balances in the S Corps books must be verified on a periodic basis to determine accuracy.

Many business owners feel as though bookkeeping should be easy enough for them to handle and usually find themselves being overwhelmed or they create messes. The delay in updates and/or messes can be costly to a business in missed opportunities, paying professionals to clean up and late tax filings

Takeaway: Bookkeeping isn't optional. If you aren't a bookkeeping pro, hire someone who is so that you can focus on what you do best.


**Payroll**

Payroll compliance, like bookkeeping, seems like something that should be easy for most people to handle. The reality is that payroll compliance is one of the most common ways a business ends up in hot water with the IRS, State and local authorities. S Corps with at least one shareholder who provides services to the S Corp must run payroll. This payroll should be run at least monthly to show compliance with reasonable compensation requirements.

Takeaway: Don't mess with payroll on your own. We recommend a third-party payroll processor.

## Tax Filings

S Corporations require annual Federal, State and Local Tax Returns to be filed on a timely basis. They are due March 15th each year or with a timely filed extension September 15th. Failure to timely file these returns comes with hefty penalties.

Takeaway: Make your S Corp tax filings a priority each year.

Accurate and timely bookkeeping with proper payroll compliance create the ability for S Corporations to file timely and accurate tax returns.

## Passthrough Entity Taxes

Many states are enacting new legislation that allows for an election to pass state income tax payments for shareholders through entities. These laws are a benefit to many taxpayers but of course require additional calculations and understanding of the legislation.

Takeaway: New laws, more available strategies, more compliance.

**Retirement Savings & Benefit Options**

S Corporations can establish the same retirement vehicles as other entity types, however, being an S Corporation shareholder-employee may result in less available profit-sharin contributions. This is because contributions are based on W-2 wages. Small wages equal small profit sharin .

Health benefits are a big topic for many S Corporation shareholders. S Corporation shareholders are not eligible to participate in an S Corporation's pre-tax health plan or some health reimbursement plans. The health insurance for an S Corporation shareholder is deductible provided the S Corporation takes the proper steps to report the health insurance premiums on the shareholder's W-2. This is another compliance piece that many S Corporations miss.

Takeaway: Take into consideration your retirement goals and health benefit needs before electing to be an S Corporation shareholder.

**Board Meetings & Corporate Minutes**

While board meetings and corporate minutes are not a requirement of S Corporations they are part of the best practices that can be of assistance in the event of legal action, taxing authority audits, etc.

It is recommended that board meetings be held at least annually, and corporation binders be updated accordingly.

**S Corporation Compliance Requirements – A Summary**

Phew. That was a lot, right? I feel like it was, so here is your compliance checklist:

1. Establish and maintain reasonable shareholder compensation.
2. Make careful and diligent decisions in regard to distributing cash and property to shareholders.
3. Establish and maintain an accountable reimbursement plan for all employees.
4. Establish and maintain basis schedules for all shareholders.
5. Establish and maintain proper loan agreements for all loans between the S Corp and shareholders.
6. Establish and maintain bookkeeping on at least a monthly basis.
7. Establish and maintain payroll compliance at a minimum frequency of every month.
8. File annual tax returns timely and accurately.
9. New state laws might be beneficial but also require more compliance.
10. Establish and maintain retirement and benefit programs with required compliance for S Corporation shareholders.
11. Bonus: Establish and maintain a corporate binder with annual board meetings and corporate minutes.

Okay—do you feel like you can handle all of that? Okay. Let's talk tax savings.

**Will An S Corp Save YOU Taxes?**

The "tax savings" from S Corps comes from a reduction in

self-employment or FICA/Medicare taxes. Historically these savings have been inflated by shareholders improperly taking very low salaries. These low salaries can create a whole host of long-range financial wellness issues. Also, with the invention of the Qualified Business Income Deduction (QBI) we are finding that fewer small businesses benefit tax-wise from forming S Corporations.

So, the big question:

Can S Corporations help save business owners taxes? Yes.

Does that mean an S Corp will save YOU taxes? That depends.

Let's look at a couple examples.

To keep things simple, in both scenarios the taxpayer is single and uses the standard deduction and has no other taxable income or deductions.

Example #1:

Our veterinarian friend from above, has a single member LLC, VetCo, LLC, which provides in-home euthanasia and end-of-life services in the Denver Metro area. They currently file the business taxes as a Sch C. They would be the only employee, and they work full-time.

The business nets $100k a year and using the many hats approach results in a reasonable salary of $80k.

Payroll taxes on the $80k are $12k and additional bookkeeping, payroll filing and tax professional costs of $4k/yr

Their effecti e tax rate is 15%.

Let's see if an S Corp election creates tax savings, or more importantly, cash savings:

| | Sch C | S Corp |
|---|---|---|
| Wages | - | $80,000 |
| VetCo, LLC | $100,000 | 7,000 |
| Total Income | 100,000 | 87,000 |
| ½ Self-Employment Taxes | 7,065 | - |
| Total Adjustments | 7,065 | - |
| Adjusted Gross Income | 92,935 | 87,000 |
| Standard Deduction | 12,500 | 12,500 |
| QBI Deduction | 16,000 | 1,400 |
| Total Deductions | 28,500 | 13,900 |
| Taxable Income | 64,435 | 73,100 |
| Federal Taxes @ 15% | 9,665 | 10,965 |
| Self-Employment Taxes | 14,125 | - |
| Total Taxes | 23,790 | 10,965 |
| Add'l Compliance Costs: | | |
| Payroll Taxes | - | 12,000 |
| Compliance Costs | - | 4,000 |
| Total Compliance Costs | - | 16,000 |
| After Tax Compliance Costs | - | 13,600 |
| Total Taxes & Compliance Costs | 23,790 | 24,565 |
| Total (Cost)/Savings – S Corp | | (866) |

In this example an S Corp doesn't save the client any money and likely will cost them time in compliance activities. Let's try another example.

Example #2:

Our veterinarian friend from above, has a single member LLC, VetCo, LLC, which is a veterinary practice in the Denver Metro area.

They file the business taxes as a Sch C. They currently have 2 additional doctors and 5 support staff as employees, and they work full-time.

The business nets $250k a year. Using the many hats approach this results in a reasonable salary of $110k.

Payroll taxes on the $110k are $17k and they already have established bookkeeping, payroll compliance and a tax professional so there would be an additional tax filing costs of $2k/yr for their S Corp tax returns.

Their effecti e tax rate is 25%.

Let's see if an S Corp election creates tax savings, or more importantly, cash savings:

| | Sch C | S Corp |
|---|---:|---:|
| Wages | $- | $110,000 |
| VetCo, LLC | 250,000 | 129,500 |
| Total Income | 250,000 | 239,500 |
| ½ Self-Employment Taxes | 12,200 | - |
| Total Adjustments | 12,200 | - |
| Adjusted Gross Income | 237,800 | 239,500 |
| Standard Deduction | 12,500 | 12,500 |
| QBI Deduction | - | - |
| Total Deductions | 12,500 | 12,500 |
| Taxable Income | 225,300 | 227,000 |
| Federal Taxes @ 25% | 56,325 | 56,750 |
| Self-Employment Taxes | 24,680 | - |
| Total Taxes | 81,005 | 56,750 |
| Add'l Compliance Costs: | | |
| Payroll Taxes | - | 17,000 |
| Compliance Costs | - | 2,000 |
| Total Compliance Costs | - | 19,000 |
| After Tax Compliance Costs | - | 14,250 |
| Total Taxes & Compliance Costs | 81,005 | 71,000 |
| Total (Cost)/Savings – S Corp | | 10,005 |

In this example there is tax savings of an amount that likely would have the client choosing to make an S Election and take on the compliance activities necessary to maintain an S Corporation.

**No Magic, Just Strategy**

The bottom line is that S Corporations aren't the magical, tax-saving unicorn that they are sold to be and making the decision to establish one isn't a one-size-fits-all solution. Back away from the crystal ball and determine your goals, needs and desires and THEN find a competent tax professional who will take all of that into account and help you achieve what you want through their expertise.

# About the Author

## Jamie E. O'Kane, CPA, CTC

 Jamie E. O'Kane, CPA, is the owner of the Colorado-based CPA firm Abundant Beans Tax & Accounting and host of The Abundant Beans Podcast. Abundant Beans Tax & Accounting provides goal-based & proactive tax strategy, tax compliance, and consulting services that make a positive impact on their client's ability to build sustainable businesses. Their niche is women-owned veterinary practices. Veterinary practice owners are changing the game in their industry, and nothing fires up the team at Abundant Beans Tax & Accounting more than helping them do it.

Jamie has been working with and advising small business owners for almost two decades. She has seen what the wrong tax advice can do to damage the longevity of a business and the business owner's goals. That is why her expertise is in balancing the proper effecti e tax strategies with compliance simplicity. The best tax strategies are tailored to the client, goal-based, proactive and compelling enough to implement and maintain.

Company: Abundant Beans Tax & Accounting
Website: www.abundantbeans.com

To learn more about Jamie and the Abundant Beans Tax & Accounting team, please visit www.abundantbeans.com.

# Myth #5
## "LLCs Make Everything Tax Free!"

## The Truth About LLCs:
## All Paths Lead to Taxation!

*By Janet M. Sienicki EA, ABA*

The question is always why? Why might a business own-er want to be classified as an LLC, as opposed to other methods of organizing the business? It is the question I ask my prospective clients, especially those clients who are considering starting a business, or perhaps changing the structure of their current business. If this question is asked and answered at the correct time, we stand a better chance that the creation of a good business structure is the result. The correct time is before an action is taken, and before mistakes are made which are difficult to change

Many clients have the misconception that an LLC elim-inates taxes. However, often the client's narrative goes like this: "About a year ago, I was talking to my friend's cousin about my exciting business idea; he said that I should be an LLC and then I wouldn't have to pay any taxes. I could not wait to get started! So, I went home and set up my LLC online. It was so easy! The next morning, I applied for a Federal Employer Identification Number, and opened a bank account. My business is doing really well. I am so glad

I made an LLC."

If we could turn back time for this misled taxpayer, we would define the term LLC, and discuss the necessity for proper legal and tax guidance in this decision making. And finally, after a thorough discussion, I would ask the client: "Why do you want your business formed as an LLC?"

**Limited Liability Company**

According to the IRS, A Limited Liability Company (LLC) is a business structure allowed by state statute. Therefore, it is important to understand that an LLC is a structure, a separate legal entity, a formation that is created, or born at the state level. A separate legal entity means that it has some of the same rights or abilities to act as a person, such as entering into contracts, having separate accountability, having the ability to sue or to be sued, or to incur debt.

Since an LLC legally exists as this separate entity, the members or owners are separated or protected from being personally responsible for the business debts or liabilities. In some states, there is forward and backward protection. For example, if our member hits someone in the head with a golf ball and is sued, the business assets are protected. The legal protection then swings the other direction, should our business be sued, our member's personal assets are protected.

This general understanding of the legal protections, as well as the legal ramifications of becoming an LLC, should be thoroughly discussed with an attorney. The discussion should include an analysis of the best state for the business to form the LLC. Since we are forming a state creation as an LLC, the legal protection, registration fees, documentation, taxes, and annual reporting fees vary from state to state. Costs must also be taken into consideration.

The main objectives must be the legal protection and structure of the business, the legal protection of the member, and making sure the LLC is the best structure for the type of business being formed. While I encourage clients to consult with their attorney to discuss the legal ramific - tions of becoming an LLC, the best decision is obtained in a joint consultation with an attorney and a tax professional. Choices made with each document being filed impact both legal and tax consequences in the future.

With an understanding of what constitutes an LLC, as well as the legal attributes pertaining to a particular business, the taxpayer must review other reasons for considering the LLC structure. For most states, the documentation required is less formal than choosing to incorporate a business. However, an LLC should have a formal Operating Agreement to define and guide the organization in its decision-making, provisions, and rules; it should be designed to assist the members in achieving the goals of the members and provide for a method of dispute resolution.

This operating agreement should be in place whether there is one member, or multiple members, because some states may have default rules which could be enacted and may not align with the wishes of the LLC. Each business that goes through the formation process will someday go through a dissolution process. A prospective LLC member should consider the filing responsibility and costs of the LLC dissolution, including the closure of accounts with all taxing authorities and the state in which the LLC was formed.

Since the structure of an LLC is by membership, rather than stock ownership, it may be less appealing to prospective investors because of the possible complexity with the transfer of ownership. This same ownership through membership is part of the uniqueness in liability protection and the sharing of profits.

Finally, the LLC decision must include a review of the taxation on both a federal and state level. The myth that our confused taxpayer presented, that "LLCs are tax free" is, of course, false. Whether this misguided business owner believed that through tax deduction, or some special LLC filing, there were no tax consequences, his belief was in error. An LLC does have the unique ability to choose how it is to be taxed, but all choices lead to taxation.

**All Paths Lead to Taxation**

Remember, the LLC was born or created as a legal entity at the state level. This entity may now choose to be taxed as a partnership (if multi-member), as a sole proprietor (if single-member), as an S Corporation, or as a C Corporation. A thorough knowledge of each of these tax classifications will allow for the appropriate choice or choices for the company in the future. A tax choice with today's knowledge and projections can be followed by a different choice when a financial situation may change. This part of the LLC decision-making and planning process requires consulting with a tax professional. An accurate projection by the owner of the estimated income and expenses for the year of start-up and at least the fi e subsequent years are crucial to choosing the taxation path of the business.

Here is an example of how the LLC owner may choose to tax the business as a sole proprietor initially, and subsequently may elect to be taxed as an S Corporation.

A client had started an LLC and chose to be taxed as a sole proprietor. She wanted the ability to take out money as it came into the business for personal use. The first few years were difficul start-up years and she had losses. It is not uncommon for a new business to experience losses in the first few years of operation. These losses were netted against other taxable income, including investment income, distributions from retirement funds, and W2 income from the job which she continued to work while running her sole proprietorship. This reduced her taxable income on her annual personal return, reducing her personal tax debt. Then, the business started becoming profitable; cash-fl w was available for the member to take a salary and cover the related payroll taxes. Being taxed as a sole proprietor became tax costly; at which point, I assisted the client with election to be taxed as a corporation, then an election to be taxed as an S Corp, which reduced her overall tax liability.

This ability to project where the business will be fina - cially, and to take advantage of multiple ways of being taxed during the life of the business, is a positive tax attribute of the LLC structure.

### LLC Sole Proprietor Path to Taxation

A single-member LLC may choose the taxation path as that of a sole proprietor. The IRS defines a sole proprietor as someone who owns an unincorporated business by himself or herself. Therefore, a sole-member LLC may choose to be taxed in this manner. The IRS considers this type of separate entity for federal income tax purposes a disregarded entity.

A sole proprietor is required to maintain accurate accounting records, including all income and expenses with supporting business receipts. A sole proprietor should maintain both a Statement of Financial Position and a Profit & Loss for accurate financial and tax reporting. It is best to maintain a separate checking account for tracking all transactions. The following story indicates how a sole proprietor believed the myth that the LLC could deduct everything for tax freedom.

A new client engaged my firm to file their personal tax return. The client had formed an LLC for his new business and was operating as a sole-proprietor. He had opened a checking account, with a corresponding debit card, for tracking all transactions, and purchased accounting software which downloaded all bank transactions. However, upon review of the client's accounting records, specifically the supplies expense, personal expenses were being paid through the business checking account. The mis-classified supplies included family groceries, pet supplies, personal care services and a sofa. The client was assuming that expenses paid using the LLC checking account would be written off as business deductions. The accounting records were corrected by including as expenses only those which were ordinary and necessary to the business. The income in the accounting records was understated because the client included only money deposited into the LLC business checking as revenue. He omitted monies not deposited into the LLC checking account. The additional cash receipts were located; they were not tax free, and they were included properly as income on the tax return.

The business owner may take funds out of the business at any time. There can be no salary. There are no W2, K-1, or 1099 forms provided to the owner. The ease of taking funds out of the business as needed is a positive attribute to the choice of sole proprietor. This choice also does not require a separate tax return from the individual's personal return. The LLC does not require an EIN, unless there are employees, other filing requirements, or banking requirements. The business income and expenses are reported on Schedule C and this net income is added to all other income on the individual's annual Form 1040 income tax return. The Schedule C is attached to the 1040.

In addition to this path leading to income tax, it increases the total taxable income, and may increase the individual tax rate, unless the business has a net loss for the year. The business income also becomes subject to both the employer's share and employee's share of self-employment taxes: Social Security and Medicare. These taxes are in addition to the income tax on the annual 1040 tax return. The increase to income, in addition to the self-employment taxes, may require the taxpayer to make federal quarterly estimated payments. Since the business is taxed at the individual level, it is taxed by its state in the same manner and state quarterly estimates may also be required.

**LLC Partnership Path to Taxation**

The IRS defines a partnership as the relationship between two or more people to do trade or business. Further, regarding an LLC, the IRS explains that a domestic LLC with at least two members is classified as a partnership for federal income tax purposes unless it files Form 8832 and elects to be treated as a corporation. A partnership requires its own checking account, maintaining all business receipts, and accurate bookkeeping including the recording of each partner's investments and distributions. The partnership funds, as deposited into the partnership checking account should be used solely for the purpose of business expenses of the partnership. A statement of Financial Position, or Balance Sheet should be maintained and may be required in the preparation of the partnership tax return.

A statement of Profit & Loss shows the income and expenses of the partnership and is used for tax reporting. Partners do not receive a W2 because they are not paid a salary. A partner can receive money from a partnership in the following ways: by taking distributions from the partnership earnings, by taking loans from the partnership which require executed notes, including well-documented terms of interest and repayment; by distributions of capital investment; or by a guaranteed distribution, which is treated as a salary on the member's tax return and is subject to self-employment taxes.

A two-member LLC being taxed as a partnership presented to me their accounting records and tax returns after several years of operating their business and self-preparing their partnership returns. One member was the sales person of the company and handled the accounting records, and the second member performed on-site services. The partners were in a disagreement over the funds being distributed to the members, the work-load division, and even over the personal expenses each member was covering out of the business checking account as needed. These personal expenditures paid through the LLC checking did not bother either member when the cash fl w was healthy, but became a problem as funds dwindled. There was no written partnership agreement, or written plan for resolving problems which tend to arise among partners.

A review of their tax returns and records indicated deductions which were not allowable. The biggest expense on the partnership return was travel. While some travel was required for the business, it was clear that this expense included personal travel. The members believed that if they had travel receipts paid through the business, all travel would be deductible.

I advised that accounting records be corrected to produce accurate tax reporting and that personal expenses of any kind could not be included as deductions on the returns. Personal expenses were not deductible just because they were paid through the partnership LLC checking account. Our meeting ended with two angry partners blaming one another for the tax and accounting mess. This LLC did not follow a plan of agreement, did not follow the law, and closed shortly after our meeting, leaving a tax mess to be cleaned up.

If the LLC chooses a partnership, it is not a taxable entity. This does not mean that there is no tax; rather the tax is imposed on the members. A partnership is called a pass-through entity because the taxable income fl ws through to the members' personal tax returns. The LLC being taxed as a partnership must apply for and secure an Employer Identification Number. The LLC choosing to be taxed as a partnership is also required to file an annual informational return form 1065.

The LLC produces, as part of this return, a Schedule K-1 which contains information for the preparation of the members' individual tax returns. Most partnerships use a calendar year-end. The tax return due date is the fifteent day of the third month following the LLC year-end. Therefore, for most partnerships, the due date is March 15 of the year following the taxable year-end.

The corresponding state partnership returns may have additional taxes; LLCs in certain states have annual taxes. It is important to understand the state filing requirements for the LLC choosing to be taxed as a partnership. For federal purposes, the LLC being taxed as a partnership is tax-free, although the partnership path leads to taxes. These taxes are paid on the member's individual annual tax returns; therefore, the share of the net income or net loss becomes part of the individual's tax planning. Members may be required to make both federal and state estimated tax payments during the year to properly pay for their tax responsibility, which is created as income is earned.

## LLC S Corporation Path to Taxation

As an LLC, the business may choose the path of being taxed as an S Corporation defined by the IRS as, "corporations that elect to pass corporate income, losses, deductions, and credits through to their shareholders for federal tax purposes." The legal entity would remain an LLC, with members not shareholders. The LLC would be required to make a timely election to be taxed as an S Corporation (S Corp). An LLC may be a new start-up or may have been taxed previously in another of the available tax structures afforded to the LLC entity, and now have the benefit to elect S Corp taxation as the business grows or evolves.

The business would be required to maintain a separate checking account, all supporting source documents, and accurate accounting records which are used to produce Statements of Financial Position and Statements of Operations or Profit & Loss statements. These statements are required for management's use to measure the financial health of the company and for tax return preparation. As an LLC choosing to be taxed as an S Corp, taking money out of the business is not as simple as the sole-proprietorship or partnership. There are various ways to take money out: payroll, distributions, member loans, and expense reimbursements through a company accountable plan. The following exemplifies how an LLC taxed as an S Corp tried to write off excess vehicle expenses.

An S Corp client, whose entity was established as an LLC, did their own accounting and brought in their records annually. Overall, they did a good job of accurately reconciling their accounting records and categorizing their cash receipts and disbursements. One year, they believed the story told to them by a car salesperson. The myth they were sold was that if they purchased a vehicle and placed it in the name of the LLC, all costs, loan interest, vehicle insurance, fuel, and maintenance were deductible by the business. The LLC member bought the story and two vehicles, one for himself and one for his wife, who was an employee of the company.

Contemporaneous mileage records were not maintained for these two new vehicles, as they believed it was not necessary as the cars were in the name of the LLC. A re-creation of mileage records from calendar entries and meeting diaries did not support the 100% deduction of these automobile expenses; actually, the percentage was substantially less. The client had not included any vehicle use fringe benefit on the member employee's W2, or the wife's W2. The client was not happy with the effect on the corporate tax return when corrected.

If the business is making money, it is imperative that there is a reasonable salary being paid to the owner before any distributions. Payroll taxes are imposed on the wages including Social Security, Medicare, and state and federal unemployment. The IRS requires reasonable compensation before distributions.

Anything less being paid as salary to the member may be considered an avoidance of paying payroll taxes. Distributions occur when checks are written to the member or transferred from the business checking account to the member's personal account. Loans to members require proper documentation, including an executed note to the business with an adequate rate of interest and repayment terms. Expense reimbursements are allowed, if the member provides substantiation for the business-related expenses under a written accountable plan which would be applied fairly to any other employee of the company.

The LLC being taxed as an S Corp does require an Employer Identification Number. S Corporations for federal purposes are pass-through entities, so the corporate return, Form 1120S, is required to be filed by the third month following the end of the tax year. This information return does not incur any tax. But this path also leads to taxation, as the member will receive both an annual W2 for the salary and a K-1 for the share of earnings and profits; the W2 and K-1 income will be added to the taxpayer's personal tax return and taxed at the individual's tax rate.

LLCs being treated as S Corporations for tax purposes need to avoid making excess member distributions as this is taxable income for the member as well. Federal and state quarterly estimated payments may be required for the member. State imposed taxes vary by state for annual S Corp tax return filings

**LLC C Corporation Path to Taxation**

Another LLC's choice of tax entity is that of a C Corporation. According to the IRS: For federal income tax purposes, a C Corporation is recognized as a separate taxpaying entity. A corporation conducts business, realizes net income or loss, pays taxes and distributes profits to shareholder.

As with all other business filings, a proper set of accurate accounting books should be maintained, including a separately maintained corporate checking account. As the sole proprietor and S Corp, the C Corporation also must be diligent to pay only business expenses through the corporate funds and be aware of the personal use of any assets for proper fringe benefit reportin .

Financial statements required for the annual tax reporting include Statements of Financial Position and Statements of Operation. As a member of an LLC being taxed as a C Corp, the money can be taken out through salary, through distributions as dividends, and through bona fide and well-documented loans to the member. The employer burden of payroll taxes on the member's salary includes Social Security, Medicare, state unemployment, and federal unemployment.

This is another choice of paths that is not tax-free for an LLC, as it leads, again, to taxation.

The LLC electing to be taxed as a C Corporation pays taxes at both the federal and state corporate level. The LLC must acquire an EIN and the Form 1120 is required to be filed by the fourth month following the end of the corporate tax year. The member-owner of the C Corp LLC will be taxed individually on the W2 income received.

A C Corporation may distribute their earnings and profits to the member. This non-liquidating distribution is dividend income to the individual owner; the profits have been taxed at the corporate level when the corporate returns were filed, and now the member who is in receipt of this distribution of the same previously taxed earnings and profits pays taxes on the dividend with the annual filing of the individual tax return.

Another distribution to the member is a return of capital. If the distribution is in excess of the member's basis, it is subject to capital gain tax treatment on the member's individual tax return. Distributions are not tax deductible for the LLC. Since the LLC incurs the tax on the profits, the company may be required to pay both federal and state quarterly estimated tax payments. C Corporation tax treatment for an LLC is a path leading to multiple levels of taxation.

**Answering the LLC question & tax-free myth.**

So, let's return to the original question... why might a business owner want to be classified as an LLC?

After reviewing the client's business discussed in the narrative, the client met with an attorney who was in agreement that the LLC was the proper legal entity for the organization, and assisted the client in drafting the Operating Agreement. The client then engaged our firm to assist in tax guidance for the decision of which tax structure would be the best for the business going forward. Although tax planning would assist the business with tax savings, the client now understands that becoming an LLC did not make anything tax free!

The client was educated in proper record-keeping for the LLC. In answering the question of why the client would want to structure a business as an LLC, avoidance of tax is not a reason, although there are tax advantages in choosing the LLC entity structure. Foremost, LLCs should be formed based upon the legal protection it affords the business and the members. If the legal structure is a fit, then it should look at both the federal and state taxation, including the flexibility the LLC choice affords the business

The cost of maintaining the LLC at the state level should also be taken into consideration. The best plan of action when attempting to answer these questions is to consult with an attorney and a tax professional for combined guidance. The taxpayer should be prepared to provide business financial projections and a business plan. Together, this team prepared with this information will answer the question of why the business should or should not become an LLC, and subsequently, how this business should choose to be taxed.

## About the Author

### Janet M Sienicki EA ABA

 Janet has over 40 years of experience in tax preparation and business account services. She has assisted businesses in their formation and the establishment of sound and meaningful accounting systems which produce financial information for both management's use and accurate tax filings. As an Enrolled Agent, Janet is licensed by the United States Treasury Department to represent clients before all administrative levels of the Internal Revenue Service.

Janet holds a BS in accounting and is an Accredited Business Advisor which requires continued profi ciency in accounting and taxation. Janet's services include business formation, accounting architecture, bookkeeping, payroll and business and individual tax preparation, planning, and representation.

Janet is a past president, vice president, treasurer and board member of the Indiana Society of Enrolled Agents and has served on various national committees with the National Association of Enrolled Agents.

Company: Janet M Sienicki LLC
Website: https://www.janetsienicki.com
Email: janet@janetsienicki.com
Phone: 219-649-0829

# Myth #6:
# "Write Off Your Wheels!"

## The Truth About Vehicle Deductions

*By Duke Alexander Moore, EA*

What's up fam! I want to talk to you about something that's been on my mind in this wild world of social media—the rampant spread of false information. It's like a never-ending floo of advice and tips, promising us the keys to success. But here's the real deal: some of these tips can lead us down a dangerous path, especially when it comes to our taxes and cars.

Imagine this scenario: you stumble across a post claiming that you can write off your entire car purchase on your taxes. Sounds incredible, right? You get yourself a shiny new ride while the government foots the bill. Well, hold up for a minute, because I've got news for you—this claim is simply not true, my friends. Falling for this myth can land you in some serious financial and legal trouble

But don't worry, I've got you! Fortunately, you've come across this chapter in the book—a guiding light amidst the sea of misinformation. Here, we're going to cut through the confusion and set the record straight. We're going to dive deep into how taxes and car expenses really work, so you can navigate the intricate world of the IRS like a pro.

By the time you finish reading, you'll have a crystal-clear

understanding—a knowledge that will keep you on the right side of the law. You'll know exactly how to make informed decisions, ensuring your financial matters are in line with the rules and regulations.

Now, here's the deal: tax laws can change faster than trends on TikTok, so it's crucial to rely on reliable sources and seek expert advice. The wisdom you'll gain from this chapter will not only save you from potential trouble, but it will also empower you to take control of your financial future

So, get ready to roll with me on this eye-opening journey. We're going to bust some myths, debunk some misconceptions, and become champions of financial responsibility. By the time we reach the end, you'll be armed with the knowledge to make smart choices and protect yourself from the perils of misinformation.

Welcome to this chapter—a safe haven of truth in the chaotic world of social media. Let's dive in, embrace our newfound wisdom, and conquer the realm of taxes and cars like true fam. Together, we've got this!

## Myth #1 Purchasing a $150,000 G-Wagon means you get a $150,000 write off

Ah, let's bust a myth that's been making the rounds, especially among car enthusiasts dreaming of owning a flas y G-Wagon. It's the idea that purchasing a G-Wagon for $150,000 will automatically save you the same amount in taxes. But here's the truth, fam—it all depends on your business use percentage.

You see, when it comes to tax deductions for vehicles, the

key factor is how much you use the G-Wagon for your business or income-producing activities. If you primarily use it for personal purposes, then unfortunately, the myth falls flat Personal use expenses typically do not qualify for tax deductions.

However, if you can demonstrate that a significant portion of the G-Wagon's use is directly related to your business, then you might be eligible for certain deductions. The percentage of business use becomes crucial in determining how much you can write off

Let's break it down: Say you determine that your business use percentage for the G-Wagon is 60%. This means that 60% of the expenses incurred, such as fuel, maintenance, and insurance, can potentially be deductible.

But here's the catch—it's not the full purchase price of $150,000 that you can deduct. Instead, you'll need to depreciate the vehicle over its useful life, spreading the deduction over multiple years. The depreciation is calculated based on the business use percentage.

So, using our example of a 60% business use, you would only be able to deduct 60% of the vehicle's depreciation each year. It's like using a coupon code that gives you a discount based on the portion of your purchase that qualifies

In essence, the myth of saving the entire $150,000 on taxes through a G-Wagon purchase overlooks the important aspect of business use percentage and depreciation rules. It's crucial to accurately assess the percentage of business use and consult with a tax professional to determine the legitimate deductions you're eligible for.

If we take the business use percentage of 60% and multiply it by the purchase price of $150,000, we can determine the portion of the vehicle's cost that may be deductible.

60% of $150,000 equals $90,000.

So, in this example, with a 60% business use, the potential write-off value for the G-Wagon would be $90,000 not $150,000.

**Myth #2 Wrapping Your Vehicle Makes it a Write Off**

Ah, let's tackle a myth that has gained some traction among entrepreneurs and business owners. It's the belief that if you wrap your vehicle with your logo or social media handle, the entire vehicle magically becomes a tax write-off. But hold on tight, fam, because it's time to debunk this myth.

Here's the truth: While wrapping your vehicle with your logo or social media handle can indeed have promotional benefits for your business, it does not automatically turn the entire vehicle into a tax write-off. It's like believing that simply slapping a sticker on your car instantly transforms it into a tax deduction powerhouse.

When it comes to tax deductions, the key factor is the direct connection between the expense and your business. Vehicle expenses are subject to specific rules and guidelines, and the same applies to the cost of wrapping your vehicle for promotional purposes.

To be eligible for a deduction, the expenses must meet the criteria of being ordinary and necessary for your business operations. While the cost of wrapping your vehicle can be considered a marketing or advertising expense, it does not automatically qualify the entire vehicle as a write-off

Here's how it works: If you use your wrapped vehicle solely for business purposes, such as making deliveries, attending client meetings, or any other income-producing activities, you may be able to deduct the portion of expenses directly related to the business use. This could include a percentage of the cost to wrap the vehicle.

However, it's essential to determine the business use percentage accurately. If you also use the vehicle for personal purposes, such as running errands or family trips, you can only deduct the expenses related to the business use portion.

So, the bottom line is that wrapping your vehicle with your logo or social media handle does not magically turn the entire vehicle into a tax write-off. It's vital to understand the specific rules and guidelines surrounding business expenses and consult with a tax professional to ensure you're properly accounting for deductions.

Remember, tax laws can be complex and are subject to change. Don't fall for the allure of a myth that promises immediate and unrealistic tax benefits. Instead, focus on understanding the legitimate deductions you can claim and keeping accurate records to support your claims.

So, while wrapping your vehicle can be a smart promotional move for your business, let's stay grounded and separate the marketing benefits from the tax implications. Drive forward with clarity, debunking myths, and making informed decisions based on accurate information.

**Myth #3 §179 allows you to fully write off your vehicle**
Let's uncover the truth about an often misunderstood concept when it comes to writing off vehicle expenses—the differenc between Section 179 and bonus depreciation. While there's a common myth that Section 179 allows you to write off the entire cost of a vehicle, the reality is different

Section 179 is a tax provision that allows businesses to deduct the cost of qualifying property, including vehicles, as an expense rather than depreciating it over time. However, it's important to note that Section 179 has certain limitations and restrictions. In the case of vehicles, the deduction is subject to a maximum limit each year, and it varies depending on the vehicle's weight and other factors.

On the other hand, bonus depreciation is another tax provision that allows businesses to deduct a certain percentage of the cost of qualifying property, including vehicles, in the year of purchase. Bonus depreciation has often been more advantageous than Section 179 because it allows for a larger upfront deduction.

Here's the catch: While bonus depreciation has allowed businesses to write off the entire cost of a vehicle, assuming it's used 100% for business purposes, starting in 2023, the deduction percentage for bonus depreciation decreases to 80%. This means that only 80% of the cost can be written off in the year of purchase.

So, to clarify, it is bonus depreciation, not Section 179,

that has historically allowed businesses to potentially write off the entire cost of a vehicle, assuming it meets the necessary criteria. However, starting in 2023, the deduction percentage decreases to 80%.

Starting in 2023, Section 179 comes with a maximum deduction limit for vehicles in the first year of ownership. The deduction limit is set at $28,900. This means that if the cost of your vehicle exceeds this limit and you wish to deduct more in the first year, you will want to explore the option of utilizing bonus depreciation.

To take advantage of either Section 179 or bonus depreciation for a vehicle, one important requirement is to use the vehicle for business purposes. Specifically, you must use the vehicle for business at least 51% or more of the time.

This business use requirement ensures the tax deductions are aligned with the intended purpose of supporting business-related expenses. The idea is that if a vehicle is predominantly used for business activities, it becomes a legitimate and necessary expense that qualifies for tax benefit

The 51% threshold serves as a general guideline to determine if the vehicle is primarily employed for business use. It signifies that more than half of the vehicle's total use is directly connected to your business or income-producing activities.

It's crucial to maintain accurate records and documentation to substantiate the business use of the vehicle. This can include mileage logs, appointment schedules, client visit records, or any other evidence that supports the percentage of business use.

**Myth #4: Writing off the entire cost is the best option**

The myth suggests that writing off the entire cost of a vehicle is always the best option. However, the reality is quite diffe - ent. In fact, there are two distinct methods for deducting vehicle expenses: the Standard Mileage Method and the Actual Method. Each method has its own advantages and considerations, debunking the notion that one size fits all

The myth goes something like this: "If you want to maximize your tax savings, always choose to write off the entire cost of your vehicle." While it may sound appealing, it's not necessarily the best choice for everyone.

The truth is, when it comes to deducting vehicle expenses, you have two options: the Standard Mileage Method and the Actual Method. Let's explore these methods to unveil the realities of vehicle write-offs

*Standard Mileage Method:*

This method allows you to deduct a standard amount for each business mile driven. The IRS sets a specific rate per mile (which can vary from year to year) that covers various expenses like fuel, maintenance, insurance, and depreciation. The advantage of the Standard Mileage Method is its simplicity. You simply need to keep track of your business mileage and multiply it by the standard rate to calculate your deduction. However, it's important to note that this method does not allow for additional deductions related to actual expenses.

The reality is that the Standard Mileage Method is the

most commonly used method for deducting vehicle expenses.

The widespread use of the Standard Mileage Method can be attributed to its ease of implementation and reduced record-keeping requirements compared to the Actual Method. Rather than tracking and documenting each individual expense, taxpayers can focus on maintaining accurate mileage logs, which serve as evidence of business use.

It's important to note that the standard mileage rate used in the Standard Mileage Method already includes an allowance for depreciation. When the IRS sets the standard mileage rate, it takes into account various factors, including the anticipated depreciation of the vehicle.

For example, in a given tax year, the standard mileage rate might be 65.5 cents per mile, and within that rate, a portion is specifically allocated to cover depreciation expenses. The exact portion for depreciation can vary from year to year (generally 26 cents/mile).

If you have a financed vehicle and make monthly payments that include both principal and interest, the interest portion is still eligible for deduction. This means that, regardless of using the Standard Mileage Method, you can separately deduct the interest portion of your car payments on your tax return.

Parking and tolls are also still deductible

*Actual Method:*

The Actual Method involves deducting the actual expenses incurred for the vehicle, such as fuel, maintenance, repairs, insurance, and depreciation. To utilize this method, you'll need to keep accurate records of these expenses throughout the year. The advantage of the Actual Method is that it allows for more precise deductions based on the actual costs incurred. However, it requires meticulous record-keeping and documentation.

When it comes to depreciation, the Actual Method allows you to calculate and deduct the actual depreciation of your vehicle over its useful life. This requires considering factors such as the initial cost, date or purchase, business miles, personal miles, and depreciation method (e.g., straight-line or accelerated) that aligns with IRS guidelines. Tracking this information accurately is crucial for claiming the correct depreciation deduction.

Now, here's where the myth gets busted: Writing off the entire cost of a vehicle may not always be the best option, even if it seems attractive at first glance. Depending on your circumstances, choosing the Standard Mileage Method or the Actual Method could be more advantageous.

Factors such as the number of business miles driven, the actual expenses incurred, and the depreciation of the vehicle should be considered when deciding which method to use. It's important to weigh the potential deductions against the effor and documentation required for each method.

Ultimately, the best approach varies from person to person and situation to situation. Consulting with a tax professional or trusted advisor can help you determine which method aligns with your specific circumstances and maximizes your tax savings while staying compliant with the IRS regulations.

**Myth #5: Commuting miles are deductible**

Reality: Commuting miles from your home to your principal place of business are generally considered personal expenses and are not deductible. The Internal Revenue Service (IRS) does not allow individuals to deduct the expenses incurred during their regular commute.

In fact, one of the key principles in determining deductible mileage is that personal commuting mileage is not considered a valid business expense. The rationale behind this is that commuting is considered an ordinary expense of daily living, rather than a direct business-related activity.

However, there is a misconception that if your home is your primary place of business, every subsequent mile driven thereafter becomes deductible. While it's true that having a home offic can have certain tax advantages, the notion that every mile driven from home onwards is automatically deductible is inaccurate.

To be eligible for mileage deductions, the travel must be primarily for business purposes. This includes activities such as visiting clients, attending meetings or conferences, or making deliveries directly related to your business. In these cases, the mileage incurred for these business-related activities would be deductible.

If your home is your primary place of business, the mileage you can potentially deduct typically starts from the moment you leave your home offic for a business-related destination. For example, if you have a meeting with a client or need to travel to another location to conduct business, the mileage from your home offic to that specific destination may be deductible.

It's essential to maintain accurate records of your business-related mileage, including dates, destinations, and the purpose of each trip. This documentation will help substantiate your deduction claims and ensure compliance with IRS guidelines.

**The Wrap-up**

Understanding the facts behind common myths about writing off your vehicle expenses is crucial for sound tax planning. While the allure of generous deductions may be tempting, it's important to adhere to the guidelines set by the Internal Revenue Service (IRS) and avoid falling into misconceptions.

When it comes to deducting vehicle expenses, the IRS requires taxpayers to substantiate their claims. This means providing adequate documentation and evidence to support the expenses being deducted. Substantiating vehicle expenses demonstrates the legitimacy of the deductions and helps ensure compliance with tax laws.

Substantiating vehicle expenses typically involves keeping accurate records, maintaining receipts and invoices, and documenting the purpose of each trip. This documentation should include information such as dates, destinations, mileage, business purpose, and related expenses. By having proper substantiation, you can demonstrate to the IRS that the claimed deductions are directly related to your business activities and meet the requirements for tax deductions.

To successfully substantiate vehicle expenses, it's essential to maintain a system for record-keeping throughout the year. This includes diligently tracking mileage, retaining receipts for fuel, maintenance, and other vehicle-related expenses, and documenting the business purpose of each trip. By doing so, you are well-prepared to provide evidence and support your deductions when it's time to file our taxes.

Consulting with a tax professional or trusted advisor can be immensely helpful in understanding the specific substantiation requirements for vehicle expenses and ensuring that you maintain accurate records. They can provide guidance tailored to your individual circumstances and assist you in navigating the complexities of tax laws.

Remember, fam, the IRS has specific guidelines in place to ensure the accuracy and legitimacy of claimed vehicle deductions. Substantiating your vehicle expenses by maintaining thorough records is essential for maximizing your eligible deductions while staying compliant with tax regulations.

By understanding the truth behind myths, following proper substantiation procedures, and seeking professional advice when needed, you can confidently navigate the world of vehicle expense deductions and make informed decisions about your tax planning.

Drive forward with accuracy, substantiating your vehicle expenses, and enjoy the benefits of legitimate deductions while maintaining compliance with the IRS guidelines.

**About the Author**

## Duke Alexander Moore, EA

 Duke Alexander Moore is a respected tax professional and content creator with well over 3.4 M followers across all social media platforms and has been featured in major publications such as CNN and Good Morning America for his savvy and easy-to-understand tax advice.

In 2018, after becoming an EA, he set up his own accounting firm, assisting small business owners and entrepreneurs with taxes and bookkeeping.

In 2020, with the aid of a popular TikTok account, Duke Tax saw huge growth and now looks after around seven hundred clients. As his business grew, Duke noticed that most CPA firms don't understand content creator taxes. Being a content creator himself he decided to transform his firm to focus primarily on content creators and entrepreneurs.

Company: Duke Tax
Website: https://www.workwithduke.com
Email: duke@duke.tax
Phone: (214) 396-6009

# Myth #7

# "A Friend Told Me to Hire 1099 Contractors to Save on Payroll Taxes"

## The Truth About Misclassifying Workers

*By Lily Tran, EA, CTC, CTP, NTPI Fellow*

The weekend was finally here, and Amir was excited to go to his friend Tom's BBQ party. While there, he met a couple who came into the kitchen to admire Tom's newly-remodeled kitchen. As the couple pointed out all the small details that made the kitchen so beautiful, Amir provided some background as to why certain design choices were made. The more they talked, the more this couple was sure that Amir was the best person to help them create their dream kitchen, but there was one problem: Amir didn't have a remodeling business; he had just helped Tom after work and on weekends. After this conversation at the BBQ, Amir decided he wanted to start a remodeling company so he could create a business built on his passion. After a few amazing remodel transformations, word was spreading fast. Amir confidently signed several new clients believing he could do them all, but client changes to the designs and delivery delays were wreaking havoc with his schedule, and he was falling behind.

## When Bad Advice Sounds Good

Amir's good friend Tom recommended that he hire some help, but Amir said he couldn't afford to pay market rates for employees because he priced his contracts low to gain more experience. Tom confirmed that having employees was expensive, and he suggested Amir hire contractors to help manage the projects, and Amir jumped at the chance to create his team without having the huge expense of hiring employees. He posted an ad on social media with the hours and rate of pay and got plenty of applications. He called everyone and found several excellent candidates, so he hired them to start right away. Amir gave them the project details, the work plans, and the tools, and supervised everyone at the various job sites.

## Cash Payments and No 1099s

At the end of each week, he calculated their pay and gave them cash, feeling proud that his business was booming and he had such a strong team to scale his operations. He had no idea that he could avoid paying employee-related taxes and cut out a ton of paperwork by just paying cash to his contractors. Unfortunately for Amir, he was misled by a myth around paying cash and not issuing 1099s, and he was breaking the law.

## An Audit Letter? I'm Not Doing Anything Wrong

One day, Amir received a letter from his state's Labor and Industries (L&I) offic  that he was selected for a state audit. Amir thought it was strange as he didn't have any employees, but he didn't really understand taxes at all.

In the book, *The Most Common Tax Mistakes Made by Small Businesses*, attorney Shawn Harju wrote a comprehensive chapter on the consequences of Misclassifying Workers, and as Amir found out, his decision to hire contractors instead of employees was a serious red flag for his state's L&I agency. Just a note that not everyone who is audited has presented red flags and sometimes audits occur randomly to ensure the tax code and compliance laws are being followed properly. Playing it safe doesn't mean you won't be audited, but in Amir's case, he wasn't playing it safe, or staying in compliance, and his actions warranted further investigation by his state's tax agency.

Instead of asking anyone for help, or hiring a professional to help him understand or deal with this matter, he simply collected the requested documents and sent them to the state. He believed it was easy to represent yourself in an audit, and after he submitted his documents, he thought it was done.

Amir is not the only one who has made this decision in scaling his business to use contractors instead of hiring employees, thinking it would be cheaper and easier. Two main reasons this idea is becoming more commonplace is the growth of an exploding gig economy where every service is for sale (often for a very low price) and easily found through a few clicks online, and the increase in government regulations protecting employees leading to more complexity and fear around liability.

**Lesson Learned**

In Amir's scenario, he quickly learned that his business wasn't in compliance with the state and federal laws. He misclassified the workers he hired to help complete his remodel projects, and this led to audit issues and payroll tax penalties. Another myth that Amir believed, which turned out to be false, was that it was easy to represent yourself in an audit. The truth is that it is best to hire a professional to represent you as you don't know the right things to say and don't understand the complex and sometimes confusing tax code including all of the rules and regulations surrounding your actions. After this long, stressful, and difficul audit experience, Amir had a better understanding of tax laws and worker classification but he would have fared much better had he not believed the myth about avoiding tax liability by just calling his employees 'contractors' in the beginning. His audit also would have been easier if he had hired a tax professional after receiving the audit notice.

**Independent Contractors versus Employees**

Over the past several years, more and more people have been seeking greater flexibility and autonomy in their work lives. Consequently, they are leaving traditional employment arrangements and embracing the idea of becoming independent contractors. As a small business owner, hiring an independent contractor means that there is a business-to-business relationship between the two parties, governed by the terms of the contract agreed upon by both parties. As a result, that contract defines the work and the relationship between the two parties, rather than the extensive employment laws that apply to employer-employee relationships. Unlike employees, independent contractors do not qualify for typical employment benefits such as health insurance, pension, life insurance, disability, paid time off, or bonuses.

**How Can Independent Contractors Help Your Company**
Hiring independent contractors allows a business owner to define and hire to meet their needs in the short term and be flexible with the terms or length of a contract. For example, a business owner might hire an independent contractor to build a digital store on the company's website, or develop a marketing campaign to announce a new product. There is a start and end to this work, and there isn't an ongoing relationship with set hours, pay, and benefits. From a taxation perspective, by hiring an independent contractor, the business owner shifts responsibility for paying federal taxes from the business to the contractor, and may not need to pay social security, Medicare, and unemployment taxes, or premiums for workers' compensation insurance. Additionally, businesses can require independent contractors to carry distinct types of insurance to protect against potential breaches of contract, which is a protection not available in employer-employee relationships.

But not all people who work for a business qualify as an independent contractor, especially if they contribute like an employee, and the IRS has definitions of the differenc between the two terms.

### Classification by the Internal Revenue Service

Amir failed to understand the difference between an employee and a contractor, but the IRS and each state's Department of Labor & Industries have clear factors to determine the right classification. For example, the IRS designed a multi-factor test to measure the degree of control and independence that exists in the relationship between the business owner and the individual providing services. The information that demonstrates the degree of control and independence for the IRS's purposes falls into the following three (3) categories:

1.  *Behavioral.* Whether the business controls or has the right to control what the individual does and how the person does his job.

2.  *Financial.* Whether the business controls the business aspects of the individual's work such as how he is paid, whether he is reimbursed for his expenses, who provides the tools and supplies to perform the work. Also, will the individual receive benefits such as a pension plan, insurance, or paid time off.

3.  *Type of Relationship.* Whether the parties have a written contract, and how long will the relationship last. Is the work being performed a key aspect of your business? Could this work be done by a contracted employee or is it a specific task requiring specifi

skills for a specific duration of time

Had Amir looked into the classification of workers before he hired anyone, he would have saved himself personal stress and tax penalties, but most entrepreneurs don't know about this important component of federal and state tax requirements.

Some questions to ask to know the difference between an employee and an independent contractor include:

1. Does the worker work for themselves and control everything about their work (when, where, how), or do they work for a company and follow the guidance of their managers, supervisors, or bosses?

2. Does the worker get to negotiate pay, hours, deadlines, and other key elements of a project or do they not negotiate every time a new project starts?

3. Does the worker submit an invoice  for the work completed and the company pays the total on the invoice without subtracting money for taxes and other fees, or does the worker get a regular paycheck with all fees and taxes already removed?

As Amir discovered shortly after starting his remodeling business, there are consequences for a business owner misclassifying workers in an attempt to cut costs or reduce the out-of-pocket expenses associated with hiring an employee. For example, the business which misclassified that person as an independent contractor may not only be required to pay the payroll taxes that would have been otherwise owed but significant interest and penalties as well. Thankfully, there are many payroll and human resource service providers like

ADP that guide small business owners through the process of setting up compensation, filling out required tax forms, and withholding tax payments automatically. Through a series of questions, the software can identify areas of your business that need special attention, such as having employees and contractors fill out the correct forms, and reminding the small business owner of the requirement for an additional form 1099 when a contractor earns more than $600 per person per year.

While these IRS guidelines can guide business owners, there may be extenuating circumstances for your business. If you believe that individuals are acting as independent contractors in your business, and you want to avoid any audit of the relationship, terms, and contracts, businesses can proactively file for an examination. Form SS-8 requests a determination from the IRS before a hiring action occurs. While this can take at least six months, businesses who are regularly hiring the same type of workers may benefit from having this determination on file. Form SS-8 can be submitted by the entity hiring the independent contractor or by the party being hired.

Once an independent contractor is hired, businesses must ensure they complete a Form W-9 to obtain the contractor's correct name and taxpayer identification number for proper documentation. Additionally, businesses must file an annual Form 1099-NEC with the IRS to report payments exceeding $600 made to the independent contractor.

## State Classification

In addition to federal requirements and tax responsibilities, businesses need to consider state regulations as well, as diffe - ent states may have their own tests to determine independent contractor status. Failure to comply with state regulations may lead to additional back payroll taxes, penalties, and interest. Even if you have determined that the person you are hiring qualifies as an independent contractor pursuant to the IRS test, you must also confirm that this person qualifies pursuant to the applicable tests of other agencies such as state agencies that regulate unemployment and workers' compensation. Since the tests may not be identical to those of the IRS, failure to do so can lead to additional back taxes, penalties, and premiums to state agencies.

## Summary

While it might seem appealing to classify workers as independent contractors to avoid certain costs, businesses must take the time to accurately assess the nature of the working relationship, comply with applicable multi-factor tests designed by state and federal agencies, and treat individuals consistently based on their designated status. This proactive approach can prevent unexpected and significant costs down the line.

## About the Author

### Lily Tran, EA, CTC, CTP, NTPI Fellow

Lily is the Founder of TaxUSign®—providing virtual tax help for whatever life throws at you™. Lily is part of an elite group of tax professionals licensed by the IRS as an Enrolled Agent (EA), a federal program authorizing her to represent taxpayers before the IRS when it comes to audits, collections, and appeals. She's a certified tax coach and a certified tax planner (CTC, CTP), as well as an NTPI Fellow.

Lily is a graduate of the University of Washington, and has nearly two decades of experience in accounting, tax, and advisory services. She is a member of the National Association of Enrolled Agents, past Director of Washington State of Enrolled Agents, and past Treasurer of Washington State Tax Consultants. She has been featured in Forbes, Bloomberg Tax and Accounting, and SUCCESS Magazine.

She is also a co-author of several other tax books, including *The Most Common Tax Mistakes Made by Small Businesses* and *Business in a Box: How to Get Tax Compliant & Financially Fit in Your Small Business*. Lily enjoys living in the Pacific Northwest with her family.

Company: TaxUSign
Website: https://www.taxusign.com
Email: hello@taxusign.com

If you would like to work with Lily and her team, please complete a client intake form on the TaxUSign website.

# Myth #8:
## "Without a 1099, My Income is Not Taxable"

## The Truth About Reporting All Income

*By Jessica Smith, EA*

Tax Myth: "I Don't Owe Taxes On My Income Because I Didn't Receive a 1099."

In the digital era, information is ridiculously easy to find

Consider how fast you can get answers to the following questions using a simple Google search:

- *What's the capital of Nicaragua?*
- *How many stars are there in the Milky Way?*
- *What is the loudest animal on planet earth?*

If we could travel far back in time, our ancestors who lived by candlelight would believe our ability to instantly access information to be witchcraft.

(And the answers are Managua, between 100 and 400 billion, and the sperm whale.)

It's astounding that we can access all humanity's knowledge through a device we can fit into our pockets

But, as it has been said, with great knowledge comes great responsibility, and I'd say that access to this knowledge in the information economy requires great fact-checking ability.

This brings me to the rising phenomenon of unsubstantiated financial advice given by people who are just not qualified

As a seasoned tax professional, I've seen lousy advice screw up the finances of ma y clients. And as social media influence gr ws, the problem will certainly worsen.

Why are people so eager to believe sensational ideas spread by media influencers? Are they really that gullible

I'd argue that nuance gets lost in the soundbites in a world that tries to condense complex information into tweets, reels, and stories. And what are taxes if not nuanced?

Those small business owners conditioned by our fast-paced media culture may have to reset their expectations about how taxes should be handled.

Tricks, "hacks," and shortcuts won't cut it. Neither will blind acceptance of bad internet tax advice doled out by online personalities.

Because here's the not-so-shocking truth—the internet is full of lies that can cause real damage to small business owners if they're not discerning enough to see through them.

The Internet Lies. A Lot.

Ah, Instagram reels and TikTok videos.

Kings of the short-form content.

Ruler of half-truths and semi-coherent thoughts.

Not to mention the epicenter of many-a-viral dance

craze.

Unfortunately, these social media platforms have also become the leading source of crappy tax advice dispensed by so-called "gurus" who share gems such as:

- *"Drain your investment accounts to invest in real estate!"*
- *"Start an S Corporation, and you'll never have to pay taxes!"*
- *"Avoid taxes by setting up a corporation in another country!"*

And, of course, there's my personal favorite, the myth I'll be addressing in this chapter:

*"Don't pay taxes on income if you didn't receive a 1099."*

Now, I can't be sure whether this terrible information comes from a place of naivety or malice.

Regardless, I'm your Tax Pro extraordinaire, here to set the record straight.

## The Big Myth

Here's a scenario I commonly see:

Carrie is a graphic designer with her own business. The IRS classifies her as an independent contractor or "self-employed." Therefore, she is responsible for paying both self-employment tax and income tax. (Reality is cruel.)

In an average year, Carrie takes on around 15 to 20 design projects from different clients. Depending on the scope and complexity, these projects pay between $600 and $10,000.

By the end of the year, Carrie will generate $106,000 in income. Go, Carrie! But unlike an individual employed by a business, Carrie is responsible for self-reporting her income and paying her taxes to the IRS so she'll need to deduct her net profit by subtracting her deductions from her gross earnings.

She's kept track of her business expenses totaling $9,000 using great accounting software.

This makes her net profit $97,000. This is the total sum on which she'll owe taxes to the IRS.

Her happy clients must send her 1099 forms stating how much they paid her throughout the year. And most of them do—except one.

The local cafe, Sunny Day Roasters, rebranded this year with Carrie's help. She created a sleek modern logo, a happy sun rising out of a coffee mug, and helped them redesign their menu. They happily paid her $8,000 (and several cups of free coffee) for her ork.

When tax time rolled around, the shop manager forgot to send Carrie a 1099 stating how much Sunny Day Roasters had paid her.

Carrie, always eager for ways to save on taxes, remembered a random bit of tax advice she'd heard from a tax advising TikTok account: "No 1099? Don't report that income!"

She reasons it's not her fault the coffee shop never sent the 1099. And besides, how will the IRS know about that income if it's not reported?

**The IRS Can Easily Find Your Unreported Income**

The first thing that Carrie (and you) must understand is this: just because you didn't send your 1099 to the IRS doesn't mean your income wasn't reported to the IRS via another method.

There are actually plenty of ways for income to get reported.

The IRS could receive a record of earning like W2s and 3rd party 1099s from businesses like Etsy and eBay, for example, and there are many more potential sources of income reporting in the digital economy.

So please, for my sanity as a tax professional, don't think you can get away with, "Oops! I never got my form! So how will the IRS ever find out?

**Is The IRS Really Watching You? Well, Maybe.**

Plenty of taxpayers underestimate the ability of the IRS to track down unreported income.

But make no mistake, despite jokes about antiquated systems and backlogs, the federal organization, which brought in about $4.90 trillion in 2022, is incredibly motivated and equipped to uncover as much revenue as possible.

At its core, the job of the IRS is to:

1.  collect money legally owed to it in the form of legally issued government taxes, and
2.  find out when taxable money is not being reported—intentionally or by way of ignorance.

But how exactly does the IRS find unreported income

## Is "Every Breath You Take" About the IRS?

Remember The Police? New Wave punk. Catchy tunes. Responsible for many-a-young-person's crush on Sting.

"Every Breath You Take" is widely believed to be a song about obsessive love. But as a tax professional, I can't help but view its lyrics through in-the-red-colored glasses.

The IRS is all-knowing and all-seeing. Yikes.

Jokes and 80's band references aside, how does the IRS know when you're misrepresenting your income on your tax return?

Turns out, they're pretty good at using their IRS sleuthing skills to figure out where a reported income doesn't match the income reported by 3rd parties.

This is the #1 reason people get flagged for audits

And once your tax account is selected for audit, IRS auditors will do a hefty deep dive into your financial personal life. They'll look at meals, travel expenses, vehicle expenses, and purchases listed as deductions to find discrepancies between your reporting and reality.

## Bank Tellers Can Flag Your Account If They're Suspicious

A common tax-evasion strategy is structuring deposits or making deposits of less than $10,000 at multiple financial institutions to avoid detection. When a deposit of more than $10,000 occurs in an account, the bank is required to fill out a CTR or Cash  ransaction Report.

To get around this, some business owners trying to avoid taxes will divide multiple deposits of less than $10,000 across different d ys or even banks.

This strategy is called "smurfing" in the industry, and it's a fantastic way to get yourself into some serious hot water with the IRS.

Bank tellers are trained to look for this behavior. If a teller becomes suspicious, they'll file a SAR, or Suspicious Activity Report, which alerts local, state, and federal fina - cial authorities of the activity.

## What Happens When The Numbers Don't Add Up?

Let's hop back over to Carrie, the graphic designer who didn't report her entire income.

She's not a sophisticated financial criminal on the prowl for tax evasion strategies.

But still, her tax account has been flagged by the IRS. Why?

The IRS is wondering why Carrie's reported income is missing $8,000. And they're especially wondering why Sunny Day Roasters LLC, who is being audited, has itemized a deductible of $8,000 for graphic design services performed by Carrie's Creative Boutique, LLC. Still, Carrie's return makes no mention of this income.

And now that they've opened this can of worms, they're ready to do a deep dive into Carrie's financial records—if necessary.

They'll likely take the most straightforward path as the

first step - sending a letter to Carrie. The letter will explain that the IRS has detected unreported income on her tax return via another reporting route—Sunny Day Roasters' itemized deductible.

Oops—Carrie realizes she's been caught misreporting income.

Luckily, the IRS letter offers her the chance to make things right by paying what she owes, plus penalties and interest.

She mistakenly believed she could omit part of her income on her tax return. Now that she's been caught, she's grateful she didn't have to pay more interest and penalties.

## Smile! The IRS is on Instagram.

When you think about the IRS, what image comes to mind?

Do you imagine an old, windowless offic with outdated PC's dotting wooden desks?

Rows and rows of crotchety accountants harrumphing over manila file folders stuffed with financial pape

While you might be right about the windowless office the IRS has been modernizing its systems and practices since the early 2000s. That includes using many social media sites as data collection tools.

So, is the IRS really spying on your Instagram account?

If your tax account has been flagged as suspicious, maybe. Especially if you're working in the entertainment industry. The IRS audit technique guide for entertainers specifica - ly instructs the auditor to "research the taxpayer on the internet." IMDB.com, Freebase.com, and "his or her own website" are all listed as fair game.

One could infer that an influencer's social media sites might qualify as "his or her own website" as well.

But don't worry.

If you're a regular guy or gal happily posting pictures of your $12 avocado toast, your friendly neighborhood IRS auditor probably isn't very interested.

What she's really looking for is evidence that the lifestyles depicted by entertainers and influencers match their reported incomes.

Because eyebrows start to raise when someone is driving a new Bentley on a $45,000 salary.

**Other Methods the IRS Has to Find Income Discrepancies**

Another way the IRS uncovers inaccurate income reporting is by analyzing loan applications.

For example, say a taxpayer decides to apply for a mortgage or auto loan and lists their income as $100,000. But their tax return shows an income of only $50,000.

Mortgage lenders use a program called the Income Verification Express Service (IVES) to confirm a potentia buyer's income during the loan application process. Once submitted, the IRS sends a record of the buyer's tax return, W-2 forms, and 1099s within a few business days.

When a loan application with a major income discrepancy is submitted to IVES, the IRS might respond with further investigation.

The IRS also uses LexisNexis, a vast data repository that houses millions of public and private records including financial assets like real-estate purchase records, property tax assessments, and deed transfer records.

Taxpayers trying to circumvent their full tax liability might omit certain assets from financial declaration. But by searching the public records available via LexisNexis, the IRS can easily uncover "hidden" assets.

## Negligence vs. Tax Fraud

Not surprisingly, some Americans cheat on their taxes.

Some cheat intentionally, while others make innocent mistakes.

But does the IRS distinguish between negligence and intentional fraud cases?

Typically. But it depends on how an IRS auditor interprets your situation.

If the auditor finds that a taxpayer hasn't fulfilled their tax obligation, they will likely impose civil fines and penalties. In the majority of cases, negligence is the reason for underpayment. This may result in a civil penalty of up to an additional 20% added to your tax bill.

If your actions are found fraudulent, however, you could face a penalty of up to 75% of the underpayment amount added to your tax bill. You could also be criminally prosecuted by the U.S. government.

And believe me, going through tax fraud prosecution

isn't only stressful for the individual involved. It can also result in long-term financial difficultie  due to penalties and legal fees.

**Protecting Yourself From Tax Problems: Mindset Is Key**

When clients ask me the best way to prevent an audit, here's my answer:

You must understand that nothing will stop the IRS from auditing you if you are selected. There is no magic formula that will render you and your financial accounts invisible to the U.S. government.

Simply put, the best thing you can do to protect yourself is:

1. Report all of your income.
2. Don't overstate your expenses.

As they used to say in the old days, honesty is indeed the best policy.

The world of frivolous social media tax advice has pushed a narrative of cheap "hacks" and fast fixes that will supposedly let you game the system without repercussion.

Sometimes it feels like "The Secret" of tax philosophy. If you just want it badly enough, you, too, can have that luxury car write-off

It's an exhausting way to think. As we move forward into a more technologically sophisticated IRS, the "legal cheat code" mentality will end in plenty of financial stress for those trying to make it work.

If you believe that by collecting fast-take tax tips and applying them to your finances, you can avoid your tax obligation, my advice is this: change your mindset.

Instead of trying to cheat the IRS with accounting gymnastics and #taxhacks, find a tax professional who truly understands the ins and outs of your business. They will help you understand the nuances of the tax code so you can legally pay as few taxes as possible.

The key word here is "legally."

It's kind of like speeding on the highway. Sure, you can drive 90 MPH, feeling on edge as you keep your eyes peeled for a radar gun.

Or, you can just drive the freaking speed limit, avoid that stress, and use your energy for better things.

Myth Busted: Yes, you have to pay tax on all of your income, even if you didn't receive a 1099.

My role as a tax strategist is to guide my clients through the complex landscape of the U.S. tax code. The goal is to help you make choices that position you and your business in the best possible place.

When you optimize your taxes with an effecti e, legal strategy, you can achieve high cash fl w while writing off as much as possible but still paying what is legally owed to the IRS.

The key to achieving this state of tax nirvana is having accurate information that is correctly applied.

This can be hard in a knowledge economy that does business in soundbites and buzzwords.

But that's where having the guidance of a qualified tax professional can be valuable.

And if I can offer you a piece of advice, it's this: Don't take tax advice from TikTok.

And one more thing.

If you're self-employed, report your dang income—even if you didn't get a 1099.

## About the Author

### Jessica Smith, EA

Jessica L. Smith, EA is a speaker and educator with more than a decade of experience helping small business owners overcome their tax problems and leveraging the federal tax code to save thousands in income taxes. As an Enrolled Agent, she has earned the privilege of representing taxpayers before the Internal Revenue Service. She is a candidate for admission to practice before the United States Tax Court as a non-attorney.

She is a member of the National Association of Enrolled Agents, the National Association of Tax Professionals, and the Idaho Association of Tax Consultants. Jessica earned a Bachelor of Science in Accounting, summa cum laude from California College.

Jessica's practice focuses on implementing tax reduction strategies and representing taxpayers before the Internal Revenue Service. In 2022, she founded The 100K EA where she guides enrolled tax practitioners through the ins and outs of resolving complex tax problems.

Company: Tax Savvy Jessica, LLC
Website: https://taxsavvyjessica.com/
Email: jessica@taxsavvyjessica.com
Phone: 619-494-1040

# Myth #9:
# "TikTok Told Me I Could Do It!"

## The Truth About Busting the Tax Myths

*By Fred Stein, CPA, EA*

I like TikTok as much as the next person. Through it, I've learned how to clean my oven, how to organize the mountains of laundry that consistently plague my house, and some really neat recipes (feta pasta, anyone?). But where TikTok can get dodgy is where it starts to dive into taxes and finances

That doesn't mean that TikTok doesn't offer some genuine advice out there—several Certified Public Accounts (CPAs) and Enrolled Agents (EAs) have accounts on there where they try to explain key concepts (NPR Money, Duke Alexander and Lorilyn Wilson are some excellent places to look). A lot of the time, however, videos that rise through the algorithm start with a false premise or a rocky understanding. And a few are downright fraudulent.

We are going to discuss some of the more popular, and persistent myths on Tax TikTok (TaxTok), and methods for deciding which are pushing something sketchy or which are authentic. In case you are unfamiliar with TikTok, it allows users to upload short videos, anywhere from a minute to up to 10 minutes. It rose in popularity during the pandemic and has become a place where dancers and singers can rise to prominence, as well as anyone else with a shtick.

The danger of this, however, is that it allows for the commodification of information. Creators need views as views translate to popularity and with popularity, the money follows. Making controversial or attractive content is one way to garner views. As we know, people don't like doing taxes—they feel obscure and burdensome. A 2015 Pew poll found that only 34% of people actually enjoy doing taxes. This dislike, along with the innate desire for the tax system to be fairer makes TaxTok attractive as it promises maximum gain for little effort

**Put It In an S Corp**
This tax myth is one of the most persistent ones. There is this idea that once something is an S Corporation (Subchapter S Corporation) that it makes everything deductible, including living expenses. Wouldn't it be nice to write off that massive grocery bill? Unfortunately, that is not quite true.

An S Corporation, or S Corp for short, is a corporation that is formed by taking a legal entity, like a limited liability corporation (LLC), and electing it to be taxed as an S Corp. It is done by filing Form 2553 and potentially a form in your state. The people who form the S Corp are known as shareholders. An S Corp is known as a "pass-thru entity". What this means is that the S Corp does not pay income tax on its profit; these are passed through to the shareholders.

There are some caveats. Some states tax S Corps on their net income—California is one of them, but New York and Texas also have a franchise tax (this is for all businesses, despite their name). States with municipal taxes, like Ohio, also tax S Corp income. But an S Corp looks attractive because of the loss of the self-employment tax.

When someone is a sole proprietor, they pay self-employment tax on their annual filin . This can be a big number—remember it's about 15% of your business income. The S Corp removes that. But it does require you to become an employee of your S Corporation and you must take a paycheck.

This can open up several benefits, which should be best discussed with you and your tax professional as there are decisions to be made based on your individual tax situation. TaxTok pushes the idea that S Corps solve a lot of problems, including allowing you to buy a vacation home, rent it, and write off your vacation there. This is simply not true.

One of the biggest rules in tax is: never put real property into a corporation. Real property are things like buildings, including homes, and land. When an individual sells these things, any gain is taxed at a more favorable capital gains tax rate, which is capped at 20%. If your S Corp sells the property, any gain is automatically taxed at 28%.

You might think—hey, I'll just re-title it in my name. Nope, that is considered a sale at fair market value and is taxable to you. Other issues include the titling of the property—is it actually in your name or in the corporation's name? That might raise insurance. But if you never titled it into your corporation's name, you may have not actually been entitled to any of the deductions you are taking. And if you take a home you own, with a mortgage on it, and put it in your corporation's name, including the mortgage, you potentially have a taxable event. You've suddenly been relieved of debt. That can be a big surprise during filing season.

TaxTok also pushes the idea that if you have an S Corp you can just take non-taxable distributions instead of wages. A shareholder is capable of taking distributions but once those distributions are higher than basis—or the value of your shares—it becomes taxable.

Susan Sample put $10,000 into her S Corp. The S Corp made $20,000 net profit at the end of the year. Her basis is now $30,000. She takes out $45,000 in distributions throughout the year. She has taken $15,000 more than the value of her basis and that is subject to tax. Not only that, her stock is now worth $0. Future distributions will most likely be subject to tax.

Additionally, the IRS is aware that people will take distributions in lieu of wages and has indicated that they will be auditing S Corps that show shareholders with distributions but no wages. Since audits are mostly chosen by computer, this is a relatively simple thing for them to program.

So when might an S Corporation be a good idea? If your annual profits are $60,000 or more, it might be something worth exploring. If you own a coffee shop and are planning on opening another, an S Corporation might offer more benefits for ou and your employees.

An S Corporation is a massive commitment, but it can also offer many perks, such as healthcare, child care benefits, and retirement benefits. Although TaxTok suggests they are easily formed and ran, every state has their own rules, on top of federal regulations. The best advice is always to talk to your tax adviser if this is something you wish to do.

**Become an LLC!**

An LLC is a Limited Liability Company, whose creation is governed by state laws. This is because an LLC is a legal entity, not a tax status. If a client comes to me and says, "I'm an LLC!" I will respond with, "Great! Now, how is your business organized?"

An LLC can be a sole proprietor, or an S Corporation, or a partnership. Its goal is to provide limited protection from an owner's assets from being taken in a lawsuit or an audit. Many videos on TaxTok talk about an LLC as a vehicle to make things automatically deductible.

A popular video on TaxTok recently just said that an LLC can pay no taxes. You can use it to write off your food, your car, your living expenses. There may be some truth to some of these—for example, if you met with a client, you could write off that Starbucks. But groceries you buy for your house and feed yourself, or your family? Where is the business purpose? No business purpose, no deduction.

The idea pushed in these videos is that if you are an LLC, everything develops a business purpose. Quite frankly, people have tried that in front of both the U.S. Tax Court and the Supreme Court and they have lost. There is a specific section in our tax code, Section 162, which says in order for a purchase to be tax deductible, it must have an ordinary and necessary business expense.

Ordinary means a purchase that is typical in your field. If you are a real estate agent, annual licensing is ordinary. So are cleaning supplies, advertising, and paying a photographer. Website costs too. If you are a plumber, tools and supplies are ordinary and necessary. You can't take apart a pipe without a wrench (or a hammer). You need to buy this tool to do your job.

Several videos also suggest purchasing a car under your LLC's name. First, this car will then be in your LLC's name, not your name, and this can raise your insurance. And it doesn't make everything tax deductible: personal use reduces those expenses and can create a taxable situation when you sell it.

LLCs may also have a state fee. In California, an LLC pays an annual $800 fee, even if it had a loss for the year. Most states have an annual LLC fee or at least minimum filing requirement. Some videos suggest forming a Delaware LLC. That might have worked in the past, but with nexus, you're most likely not avoiding your state's filing requirements.

You don't need to be an LLC to take deductions for your business. As long as they are ordinary and necessary, and you have a clear business goal (ex: cleaning houses, building houses, running a restaurant), then the deductions are legitimate.

Should you become an LLC? That's a great question! An LLC can allow you to maintain a separate bank account (for ease of organizing your expenses) and keep your business separate from your personal. It does provide limited protection. But with most things, you might want to chat with a tax professional before pulling the trigger. Depending on your business, the benefit might not outweigh the reporting and annual costs.

### Make Everyone a 1099!

This idea is attractive because you save on payroll taxes. This passes that responsibility on to the person you just hired. You may want them to be a contractor, but the IRS, and the Department of Labor (and states like Texas and California) have very definite ideas of what is a contractor and what is an employee.

The difference between an employee and a contractor comes down to:

- **Financial Control:** Are there unreimbursed expenses? Who provides the tools and the space for the work? Is the time when someone is required to work set by the payer or by the person providing the services? How frequently is the person paid?

Who provides workers compensation/liability insurance?

- **Behavioral Control:** Does the payer control when and how the work is being done, through instructions, training, or other means?

- **Party Relationships:** Is there a written contract or an oral agreement to the work? Does the payer provide access to benefits, such as a pension plan, vacation pay, or sick pay?; how long does the contract last; and are the services provided a key part of the regular business of the company?

Susan Sample is an architect. She draws up plans and meets with clients. She is contacted through her website. ABC Construction Corp often hires her for their projects. There is a written contract specifying the work, the timeline for it, and the pay. Susan then completes the work when she wants and, as long as it's delivered by the deadline, she will be paid. She has an offic  for which she pays rent and she provides her own software. In this case, Susan is a contractor.

Elliot Example is also an architect. He goes into the ABC Construction Corp building daily for work. He has an offic  there and ABC provides his drawing station, his software, desk, and coffee in the break room. He has a supervisor with whom he meets. Elliot is an employee.

But what if ABC made a space for Susan to work so she could access their software for a specific subject? What if they met with her regularly? Is she now an employee?

In some states, like California, she might be considered an employee. You may decide, however, that you don't want to deal with payroll and make Susan a contractor. Susan, or any taxpayer, can meet with a labor attorney, or a competent tax pro, who might review the controlling factors with Susan and tell her she was an employee. Susan can file a form with her taxes, telling the IRS that you are liable for her FICA taxes, and file a complaint with the Labor department.

Determining your relationship with any future workers, and the state laws governing it, can help avoid these situations. A contractor completes a Form W-9 before they get started. An employee will complete a Form W-4, an I-9, and then whatever state withholding form is required. These forms should be retained for four years. With the rise of online software programs like Gusto, setting up and paying someone is easier and much more streamlined.

If you are unsure whether a job you are offering is for a contractor or an employee, consider calling a labor or employment attorney and/or a tax professional.

### Be Exempt!

There is a very popular video on TaxTok of a woman claiming that one can be exempt from federal taxation by marking exempt on their Form W-4. This means an individual is now no longer required to pay federal withholding taxes.

Now this particular video has been stitched and debunked by many professionals, but in case you didn't see it, marking yourself exempt on a W-4 is going to lead to a whole lot of pain come next April.

The purpose of the W-4 is to estimate how much in taxes should be withheld from your earnings. IRS offers a paycheck withholding estimator to help you determine your correct withholding in order to reduce any liability come filing time

During tax season, you report what you made, and Congress allows you some deductions to find your taxable income from which your tax is determined. Then you look at payments you made, either withholdings from your paychecks or estimated tax payments. If you were marked exempt, there were no withholdings and you will owe. Quite possibly a lot.

Additionally, if an individual owes over $1,000, they will receive an underpayment penalty. Let's say, you made $50,000 as a single person, your tax liability is $4,500, and you have no taxes withheld, then you will owe that $4,500 plus a penalty. This is a large amount to owe all at once. Additionally, you will need to adjust your withholdings quickly to stop this from happening again.

There are other ways to reduce your tax liability and a meeting with a tax pro can review your options. There are health savings accounts (HSA), tax deferred retirement plans, and tax shifting for which you may be potentially eligible. It's always better to discuss things first before diving into it. This can help you to avoid being hit with penalties or additional taxes when you file  our taxes.

## Put it in a Trust

This one has really gained traction. The idea is that you put all of your income and your assets (car, home) in a trust and then you pay yourself out of it. Trusts aren't taxed and your income isn't taxed, and you can make gifts as deductions (ex: you gift yourself money out of the trust). Or, because you don't own anything anymore, you can't be taxed on it (there is also this argument that the government can't tax entities, which is not true as the government taxes S Corporations and partnerships and trusts just fine)

Let's break this down bit by bit. A trust is formed under state law and is a financial agreement that allows a third party, called a trustee, to hold assets on behalf of a beneficiary or beneficiaries. There are many types of trusts—a grantor trust, or living trust, which doesn't file an annual return, but upon your death, will hold all your assets, potentially helping to avoid probate; an irrevocable trust, which cannot be changed; and a charitable trust, which allows certain benefits to go to a charity and others to beneficiaries. Since trusts are governed by state law, it's always best to consult an attorney first before setting one up and to ensure all proper filings are done in the county recorder's offic

The second part is about putting all of your assets into a trust and suddenly there is no more taxable income. Well, this goes back to what kind of trust. Did you use a grantor trust? That doesn't exist on its own until you're dead, so it still pays taxes. If you put your house in your trust's name, depending on the type of trust, you may still file taxes. A complex trust? You absolutely have to file a trust form, called a Form 1041, and only certain expenses are deductible. A broken water heater may not be if it's for the maintenance of an asset (however, it can be added to basis at sale time).

The third part is about giving gifts and making those non-taxable—like most things, it depends. Some of the fast rules about gifting is the giftee rarely pays taxes on the gift; that the donor must file a tax return if the gift is over a certain amount; and depending on the gift, you may be subject to state and local taxes. For example, Grandma Jones gives her granddaughter $20,000 for university. Grandma gave over $17,000 the 2023 limit on annual gifts. She will need to file a gift tax return. However, because the total amount of gifts that someone is allowed to give is closer to $12 million, that means Grandma Jones can give up to $12 million without triggering a gift tax.

But let's say Grandma Jones gives a house to her granddaughter. Depending on the value of the house, she may need to pay a local sales tax and any titling costs. Additionally, gifts are never tax deductible. If Grandma is giving her granddaughter $20,000, then she cannot deduct that on her return. (There are options here to avoid the gift tax— Grandma could have set up a 529 plan or given $10,000 to a parent and then $10,000 to her granddaughter, and thus avoid the gift tax filing altogether. However, if she is giving to her children, she may run up against the $17,000 limit.

If a trust is paying people, say $30,000 a year, as the video goes, they are going to need to file a gift tax return. That gets added up so by the time they stop, they may have reduced their ability to give more gifts closer to the end of their life. They also cannot deduct this $30,000 from the trust.

Finally, you can live off of your trust and have no taxable income. That's a nice idea, but if the trust is consistently putting money into your personal bank account, that's going to flag a couple of things. First off, a state is going to notice you're not paying taxes. Secondly, banks are subject to anti-money laundering reporting. They may see these as suspicious activities and file a report with the enforcement arm of the IRS. Thirdly, under the law, all income that you receive is taxable, unless somehow exempt. This does not qualify.

Now, trusts can have some excellent benefits. They can help you manage and protect assets and potentially save your beneficiaries from probate court upon your death. They will not simply make everything tax free though.

**Get that Mercedes!**
Another series of videos push this idea that there is a secret IRS code section, called Section 179, and you can use it to write off your car, including a luxury car like a Mercedes Benz or a Hummer. Some of these videos say that you can

get a new car every year and others say you need an S Corporation to take advantage of this benefit

Section 179 has been around for over sixty years, but it really rose into prominence after the Great Recession as a way to stimulate the economy. It is an election to take an accelerated deduction off an asset's cost. A car, like a computer or a tractor, which has a business use is an asset, and every year you take a small amount for depreciation (computers generally are no longer depreciable. Just deduct that!).

Section 179 allows you to write the whole thing off. Bought a new Toyota for $30,000 for your business? Instead of taking $6,000 a year over the fi e year life of the car, you can elect to take it all at once! That is Section 179, and it is an attractive benefit, depending on your business's income and the nature of your business.

You do not need to be an S Corp to take advantage of Section 179. You just need a clear business purpose, much like with not needing an LLC to take business deductions.

However, if you take Section 179 you reduce the value of that car to $0. So, let's say you buy a Benz for $60,000 and you take Section 179. On a tax return, it's now worth $0. If you sell it the next year for $50,000, you now have $50,000 in taxable income. Any time you sell or dispose of a business asset, you must report it (and the IRS does track it, as does your state, especially through sales and title transfer taxes).

Additionally, there are limits on those luxury cars under Section 179. The vehicle has to have a weight of at least 6,000 pounds but not more than 14,000 pounds. The deduction is limited based on weight, with $28,900 for certain vehicles in 2023. Amounts that are unused can carry over to the next year. These vehicles must also have more than 50% business use and it must be in business use by December 31st of the calendar year to be eligible.

The total amount of Sec 179 a person can take is much higher, close to over one million, but autos have limits.

Let's say that Susan Sample purchased an SUV for $60,000. She uses it 80% of the time for business. Her deduction is limited to 80% of the $60,000 or $48,000. But because it's an SUV, it's capped at $28,900.

You might think—well, I'll just make it 100% use. This is OK if it's a truck that stays in a business lot and you don't drive it home. But if you use it to pick your kids up from school, or to visit friends, or travel, that is not a business use and reduces the 100%. Additionally, if you take Section 179, you cannot take it on a car for which you use the mileage deduction; you will need to accurately track your gas, repairs, insurance and other expenses. This is because the mileage deduction already includes depreciation in it.

There also needs to be a necessary business reason. A doctor who drives back and forth from her practice doesn't necessarily need a Hummer as you can't deduct commuting (traveling to and from home and an offic  is commuting). What is the use? Now, if it is the doctor from the popular series *Virgin River*, then perhaps a Hummer may be necessary as the doctor there drives into the mountains and long distance to rural areas. It may be beneficial in that case.

A contractor who builds homes and needs a truck bed that can haul a ton of bricks and wood? Sure, that giant Ford F150 would seem necessary. A real estate agent who needs a brand new Mercedes every year to impress her clients? It depends! If she is working in Silicon Valley or Highland Park, Texas, then she might need it as these are high-income areas. But if she is not, then it may not fall under 'necessary.'

Some states also impose limits on Section 179. California only allows $25,000 maximum each year and Ohio and Kentucky have very specific formulas for percentages of Section 179 (Ohio requires add backs!). I spend a lot of time, especially toward the end of the year, discussing Section 179 and its tax implications with clients, so don't be afraid to call up your tax professional. Section 179 should be a deliberative election, and not a way to spend money or try to gain a write-off at the end of the  ear.

**You Talk about Tax Pros a Lot**

Absolutely, and it's not just because I am one. Taxes can feel like simply filling out forms, but those forms come from the extremely complex tax code found in Chapter 26 of the U.S. Code, along with the state and local counterparts. Taking an individual's life and fitting it into a tax code isn't easy; this isn't one-size-fits-all. It involves looking at the law and assessing your situation and seeing how the tax code applies. We don't make the tax code, we just make a living understanding that code and applying it in the most beneficial, and legal, w y for our clients.

For example, our real estate agent in California. I might have a different conversation with her about whether an LLC is a good idea, as opposed to someone in Ohio. Ohio only has a small LLC set-up fee and no real annual requirements; California has an $800 annual fee. Is my client making enough money to justify this? Or is this a side gig, where she's selling maybe a house or two a year and $800 is a big hit to her income stream?

What if my client wants to set up a trust? First, I would advise them to meet with an attorney, but I would also discuss what the tax implications might be. If I have a client taking care of an elderly parent through a long-term care facility, I might mention an elderly care or Medicaid asset protection trust. And if my client wants to be an S Corp, I would work with them to review all of the potential issues, such as how it will affect the qualifying business income deduction, how payroll will affect their individual return, and how their bottom line might look.

Because your tax situation and your life is fluid and not a hard line, tax answers often don't fall into absolutes. This is why tax professionals say "it depends" frequently (and frustratingly). I might not recommend a traditional IRA for a high net worth individual because that is pre-tax income and, if they have a retirement plan through work, it may not even be a deduction! Like dominoes, one tax decision can affect others and knowing how those interrelate is a key part of the advisory services that a tax pro does when answering your questions or working on your return.

There are tax professionals on TikTok who push back against some of these loose interpretations of the law while also offering expert advice, including Lorilyn Wilson, CPA (@thenotspicyaccountant), Jason Staats, CPA (@jstaatscpa), Duke Alexander Moore EA (@DukeLovesTaxes) or Ron Parisi, CPA (@cpa_on_fire)

If you don't have a tax professional, you can easily find a designated EA or CPA by visiting the IRS's directory of federal tax return preparers. Please ensure their credential is current and if they are familiar with your area. TaxTok videos can open a conversation with your tax pro to discuss strategies to legitimately reduce your tax liability, but it is your tax professional who has the expertise to keep you compliant with the tax code.

## About the Author

### Fred Stein, CPA, EA

 Fred Stein is a CPA and Enrolled Agent with several decades of experience in both accounting and tax fields.

Although he came to it later in life, Fred has embraced his bi-coastiality. When he's not costuming his cat for TikTok videos, he keeps quite busy with his blogs "Avoca-Don't" and "I'm Achin' for Some Bacon." Fred has been the fearless leader of the BQ Tax & Accounting team since 2007.

Company: BQ Tax & Accounting Ltd
Website: https://www.bqtaxpro.com/
Email: info@bqtaxpro.com
Phone (518) 234-4829

# Conclusion

Every business owner wants to build a thriving business and reap the rewards of their hard work and dedication. They put in countless hours creating the best products or services, and spend much of their time on operations, sales, and marketing. Savvy small business owners hire professional tax and finance experts to be a guide in their business, helping them navigate tax laws and regulations, and stay in compliance and up to date with their tax responsibilities. Other small business owners might not build a finance or tax team, which means they might rely on personal experiences from friends, or news articles and short videos for tips and tricks to manage their taxes. This is often where tax myths are born, and why this book is so important.

Our mission in creating this book is to provide every small business owner with a valuable resource so no one is making misguided, misinformed mistakes in the areas of taxes and money matters. Every author in this book wants to help you take ownership of your success, today and in the future with actionable, accurate advice. We don't want to see you stressed, strained, or struggling, which is why every chapter breaks down another myth we see in the marketplace. We want you to start with the right structure, set up the best systems, and take advantage of the right allowances so you can reduce your tax payments and keep more money in your business (and in your bank account) without breaking any laws.

By thoroughly explaining the top tax myths many small businesses make, we are giving you the shortcut to successful tax and regulatory compliance. If you can avoid falling for these myths in your business, you have a better chance of being strong, healthy, and thriving.

We see this over and over across every industry: being the expert in your business and in your industry empowers you to be a leader with a success story. However, you don't have to master every part of your business to be at the top of your game; successful people surround themselves with a support team who are experts in their fields, working together for great rewards. All of the contributing authors in this book work with small business owners just like you to help them avoid the most common tax myths that cost time, money, and peace of mind. These professionals are here to partner with you and support your business growth, so don't hesitate to reach out with any questions.

Printed in the USA
CPSIA information can be obtained
at www.ICGtesting.com
LVHW011338010524
778880LV00013B/717